Margaret Boden is Reader in Ph
University of Sussex. Born in Lo
scholar at Newnham College, Ca
class honours in both natural scie
and a Harkness Fellow at Harvard   ool where her
adviser was Jerome Bruner: she gained a PhD in social psychology,
specializing in cognitive studies. She lectured in philosophy at the
University of Birmingham from 1959 until 1965 when she went to
Sussex. In 1979 she was visiting cognitive scientist at Yale
University.

Dr Boden's previous books are *Purposive Explanation in Psychology*
(1972) and *Artificial Intelligence and Natural Man* (1977).

Modern Masters

Piaget

Margaret Boden

Fontana Paperbacks

First published by Fontana Paperbacks 1979

Copyright © Margaret A. Boden 1979

Set in Pilgrim

Made and printed in Great Britain by
William Collins Sons & Co. Ltd, Glasgow

A hardback edition of *Piaget* is published by
Harvester Press

For Marie Jahoda and Solly Jacobson

Contents

Acknowledgments

I am very grateful to the following friends for their helpful comments on the draft, and hope they will not be held responsible for any faults that remain despite their advice: George Butterworth, Roy Edgley, Brian Goodwin, Marie Jahoda, Mike Scaife, Aaron Sloman and Neil Warren.

'There's no use trying,' said Alice: 'one *can't* believe impossible things.'

'I daresay you haven't had much practice,' said the Queen. 'When I was your age, I always did it for half an hour a day. Why, sometimes I've believed as many as six impossible things before breakfast.'

Lewis Carroll

I noticed with amazement that the simplest reasoning task . . . presented for normal children up to the age of eleven or twelve difficulties unsuspected by the adult.

Jean Piaget

My theory of development, which is particularly concerned with the development of cognitive functions, is impossible to understand if one does not begin by analysing in detail the biological presuppositions from which it stems and the epistemological consequences in which it ends.

Jean Piaget

An organism is a machine engaged in transformations.

Jean Piaget

A list of the abbreviations used for Piaget's works can be found on pages 167-70.

1 Piaget the Polymath

Jean Piaget is world-famous outside his native Switzerland for his work in child psychology, but he is not primarily a psychologist. He calls himself a 'genetic epistemologist', a label that can act as a reminder of his intellectual priorities. He is a biologist and philosopher (more strictly: an epistemologist) first, and a developmental psychologist only second.

This is not a matter of recognized intellectual achievement, for it is in psychology alone that Piaget has been outstandingly influential. His children Jacqueline, Lucienne and Laurent are immortalized as babies in the psychological literature. Piaget's imaginative and detailed studies of the development of thinking, from babyhood through infancy to adolescence, have inspired countless admiring followers and respectful critics. And psychologists have given much attention to his theory of intelligence as interiorized action, to his vision of the mind as a continuously developing system of self-regulating structures that actively mediate and are transformed by the subject's interaction with the environment. Even his fiercest critics – who reject his theories, question his data and censure his methodology – allow that he has drawn attention to a wide range of important psychological questions. His influence has not been confined to academic psychology, but is seen in educational practice also: radical revisions of school curricula and classroom organization (toward greater reliance on the child's spontaneous learning by way of concrete activities and self-regulation, and less on early reading) have been recommended on the basis of his ideas. In 1969, at the age of seventy-three, he was the first European to receive the Distinguished Scien-

tific Contribution Award of the American Psychological
Association, which commended his work as 'a unique and
lasting monument in the psychological literature'.[1] By contrast, although some philosophers and a few biologists
value his ideas, many others (whether justifiably or not)
do not even read him.

Nor is this fact (that Piaget is not primarily a psychologist) simply a matter of chronology with respect to academic training or guiding ideas, although the point does
stand as a statement of Piaget's intellectual biography.
He was initially trained as a biologist, and received his
doctorate in 1918 for a thesis on molluscs. His first publication (in 1907, at the age of eleven) reported his sighting
of an albino sparrow, and while still a schoolboy he was
curator of molluscs at the Natural History Museum in
Neuchâtel. By the age of fifteen he was publishing notes
on the variation of pond snails, and his experiments on
adaptation in pond snails (and a similar series on plants)
were to continue through middle age. Even in his teens,
he was arguing for evolutionary views opposed to the
orthodox Mendelian position – which sees chance genetic
mutations as the motor of evolution – and claiming that
biological (and epistemological) structure is an indestruct-
ible, though progressively modifiable, feature of the
organism (and of its knowledge). He described this structural modification as occurring by way of assimilation and
imitation (later termed 'accommodation'), ideas drawn
from F. Le Dantec which were to evolve into key concepts
of Piagetian psychology.

Piaget's nascent philosophical interests were stimulated
by L. Sabatier's 'evolutionary' account of religion and
by H. Bergson's *Creative Evolution*, which discussed issues
concerning the biological problem of adaptation that had
already captured his attention. In addition, it seemed
relevant to the young man's search for a reconciliation
between scientific knowledge and religious values, enabling him 'to see in biology the explanation of all things

and of the mind itself.' [A 240] He decided then 'to devote [his] life to philosophy', soon 'specializing in biological philosophy', [IIP 5 & 7] and so read philosophy and logic avidly while continuing his biological studies. Piaget's first book (written during the First World War) was not a psychological study but a philosophical prose-poem about war, which forecast a growth of knowledge reconciling science, socialism and Christianity. His second (in 1918) was a philosophical novel, of a largely autobiographical nature, recounting a young man's intellectual crisis in the search for true knowledge, whether scientific or moral. Beginning from the biological problem of the adaptation of species, the hero finds his intellectual resolution (and spiritual salvation) by way of the concepts of equilibration and the circle of sciences, each of which came to prominence in Piaget's later writings. [A 243; G 26-37]

His psychological studies did not start seriously until 1919. After receiving his doctorate in biology at Neuchâtel, Piaget worked in psychological institutions in Zurich and Paris. His initial interest was in psychoanalysis and clinical psychiatry, but in 1920 he was asked by one of the founders of intelligence testing to help in the routine standardization of the tests. Piaget soon found himself more interested in the quality of the children's errors than in the quantity of their correct responses. These errors were not mere insignificant mistakes due to childish ignorance and uninformed guessing. Rather, they suggested — to Piaget's amazement — that the logical structures of the child's mind are importantly different from those of adult knowledge. On the biological principle that ontogeny may provide clues to phylogeny, Piaget decided to explore children's thinking for the light it might throw on the nature and development of human knowledge in general: psychology, he thought, is 'the embryology of intelligence'. [A 245] He was encouraged also by the child psychology of J. M. Baldwin (who coined the phrase 'genetic epistemology'), and by the work of Freud — who not only stressed developmental issues, but used apparently anomalous behaviour as a clue to the underlying generative structures of the mind.

Piaget intended his foray into psychology to last only five years, but instead it lasted over forty. [A 255] Even so, he never entirely deserted biology and philosophy for psychology; and in his old age he returned to his original plan. He now concentrates on biological and epistemological writings that draw on his discoveries in developmental psychology, while also supervising the continuing programme of experimental research at the International Centre of Genetic Epistemology in Geneva.

The crucial point is that Piaget did not take up psychology for its own sake, but as a means to the end of developing a biologically oriented theory of the nature and origins of knowledge: 'Between biology and the analysis of knowledge I needed something other than philosophy . . . a need that could be satisfied only by psychology.' [A 240] In his first systematic account of his psychology, thirty years later, he still identified his main aim as being to unify biology and logic; [PI 3] and this claim continually recurs in his current writings. Moreover, by 1919 the problem and the main conceptual outlines of his answer had already been suggested by his biological studies. His basic concern was the adaptation of living things to their environment. As a special case of this biological problem, he was led to consider the phenomenon of human knowledge, especially that knowledge (logic and mathematics) which seems to transcend the limitations contingent upon our spatiotemporal embodiment. And even in his earliest writings, Piaget was already describing adaptations in terms of the now familiar notions of self-conserving (later: 'self-regulating') structures, developing by equilibratory processes of assimilation and accommodation.

Biology, epistemology and psychology have different approaches to knowledge, each of which is employed by Piaget. The biologist asks: How does knowledge contrib-

ute to the adaptation of the organism to its environment,
and how has it evolved throughout the phylogenetic scale?
The epistemologist asks: How is knowledge possible, and
what types of knowledge are basic to, or essential for our
(or any) view of reality? And the psychologist asks:
What sorts of knowledge does the (human) organism have,
and how do they develop from birth to maturity? For
Piaget, as we shall see, not only does the answer to each
of these questions influence the answer to the others, but
there are significant conceptual parallels between the
various answers. Being similarly structured, the answers
can be developed, or argued for in similar ways.

Piaget's characteristic method of argument is dialectical
in form, and he sometimes refers to his position as 'dialectic constructionism'. [BK 212] A dialectical argument
passes from the *thesis* to its contradictory *antithesis*, and
thence to the *synthesis* – which in turn can act as a new
thesis begetting a novel synthesis on a higher level. Each
synthesis transcends the two prior opposed statements, in
that it retains their insights but avoids the contradiction by
a reformulation of the problem that rejects one of their
shared assumptions and so escapes the conceptual limitations it imposed. The progression from level to level is not
a linear sequence wherein one statement implies a second
which implies a third, given background premises that
either are fixed or which vary independently of the statements concerned. Rather is it a spiralling creative process,
wherein the context of background premises is itself
successively reconstructed, because of the interaction between thesis and antithesis at each new synthesizing level.
As we shall see, Piaget views psychological (and biological)
development similarly as an 'epigenetic' spiral, not a pre-
determined unfolding of innate properties (whether
through psychological maturation or environmental trig-
gering). So the 'developmental' flavour of dialectical reasoning might be expected to appeal to Piaget, and he regards
dialectics as 'inherent in all the [social or natural] sciences

involving an evolution or becoming', as well as being an important mode of thinking in philosophy. [IIP 115]

Accordingly, Piaget argues dialectically in dealing with the questions about knowledge that were noted above. His view of them as, essentially, one and the same question is reflected in the identical dialectical structure he discerns in the theoretical traditions of the three disciplines. In psychology, the thesis, antithesis and synthesis respectively are typified by behaviourism, Gestaltism (and ethology) and Piagetian developmental psychology. In philosophy, they are represented as empiricism, rationalism (including phenomenology) and Piaget's genetic epistemology. And in biology they appear as Lamarckism, Darwinism and his preferred theory of 'evolution by epigenetic assimilation'. In each of these cases, he says, the thesis posits *genesis without structure*, the antithesis posits *structuralism without genesis*, and his own synthesis offers *genesis with structure*, or a 'genetic structuralism' that focuses on the self-regulated development of increasingly equilibrated structures. [e.g. 6PS 145]

A continual equilibration is thus said to be central to developmental processes of all kinds (including dialectical thinking itself). It is the resultant of two polar opposites, each of which is present to some degree in every interactive change: assimilation and accommodation. Assimilation is the modification of an incoming stimulus, or input information, by the activity of a pre-existent structure. Accommodation is the active modification of the structure itself, so as to adapt to the input. And equilibrium is a relatively stable (but inherently dynamic) state of some structure, such that it can accept and adapt to varied input without any essential change. Since equilibrium is neither perfect nor permanent, eventually some input will defeat the assimilative and accommodatory powers so far developed by the existing structure. If it is to deal with (assimilate) the input, rather than ignore it, further structural development must take place; this is an accommodation of a more radical type, leading to equilibrium on a higher structural level.

Piaget uses these abstract terms to cover developing structures of all kinds. Examples within their initial, biological context include the accommodation of the pupil to light, the assimilation of food by the digestive system, and the homeostatic equilibrium of blood temperature. Like the Genevan psychologist E. Claparède, who described adaptive behaviour in terms of homeostatic equilibrium, Piaget widened these notions of biological self-regulation to include psychological instances. And he applied them to all stages of intellectual growth, from the newborn baby's learning to suck to the adolescent appearance of logic. For instance, the baby assimilates her teddy's ear to her capacity (or 'sensorimotor scheme') for sucking, so that she can deal with it in one of the few ways she knows; her mouth accommodates differentially to nipple or teat so that she can suck milk; and her sucking ability is equilibrated when she can recognize suckable objects reliably and suck them firmly. Examples like these are relatively clear. When it comes to logical (or 'operational') thinking, Piaget applies his notion of equilibration in a more abstract – and more problematic – manner. For instance, he uses it to account for the appearance and adaptive value of reversibility, wherein an action (whether physical or intellectual) is understood by the child to be potentially undoable, so as to restore the original state of affairs. In such cases, one may feel that the term 'equilibrium' names, rather than explains, the adequacy of adaptive activity.

It is because the dialectical processes of equilibration comprise the active building of structures that Piaget calls his theory 'dialectic constructionism'. Activity is a crucial Piagetian idea, in two main senses. First, he believes that it is only by way of the baby's overt (bodily) actions and the older child's internalized (mental) actions that knowledge of objects – whether actual or hypothetical – is possible. And second, his view is that knowledge and learning are not so much discovery as construction: the active creation of novel structures that did not previously exist – either in the world or in the mind. Empiricist and rational approaches to psychology and epistemology are both inadequate, since the first ignores activity and structure entirely while the second posits active structuration without paying attention to 'the logical procedures or natural processes by which the whole is formed.' [S 9] For Piaget, a child who puts pebbles in a straight line, arranges sticks according to length, or sees a ball as the cause of a broken window, is creating order rather than finding it waiting in the world; but she could not have done these things without a long process of bodily and mental activity whereby the various intellectual structures of ordering were themselves constructed.

Structure, too, is a crucial Piagetian idea. Biological structures, or wholes, caught his attention in his youth, and he says that 'If I had known at that time (1913-15) the work of Wertheimer and of Kohler, I would have become a Gestaltist.' [A 242] His own psychological concept differed from the Gestaltists' in stressing the development of structures, and has become increasingly formalized in terms of logical or algebraic definitions. Latterly, with the rise of structuralist movements in linguistics, mathematics and anthropology, he has described his theory as an instance of structuralism in general. [S] (It has been said that 'structuralism is the opium of the polymath', and those who tend to agree may be tempted to dismiss Piaget accordingly; for reasons which I hope will become clear, this would be a mistake.)

The three key ideas in Piaget's notion of structure are wholeness, transformation, and self-regulation. A structure is a unified *whole* whose parts can be identified only in relation to each other and their place in the overall structure. For Piaget, structures are dynamic, both in their development and self-maintenance. And structural alterations are not simple or random changes, but orderly *trans-formations*, whereby one structural form or set of relations is succeeded by another. It is only by way of active transformations that knowledge is possible:

> In order to know objects, the subject must act upon them, and therefore transform them: he must displace, connect, combine, take apart, and reassemble them. From the most elementary sensorimotor actions (such as pulling and pushing) to the most sophisticated intellectual operations, which are interiorized actions, carried out mentally (e.g. joining together, putting in order, putting into one-to-one correspondence), knowledge is constantly linked with actions or operations, that is, with *transformations*. [H 704]

Finally, structures are *self-regulating*, or autonomous, in that the nature of the whole is conserved by adaptive compensatory transformations among the parts. Perfect conservation is not always achieved (so embryonic self-regulations can generate a monster). But logico-mathematical structures are 'closed' under all possible transformations, such that no item can be generated that is not a meaningful element of the structure concerned. (Add and subtract integers, and you can get from any one to any other in indefinitely many ways, without ever generating a fraction.) Piaget sees this feature as due to a perfect equilibration, which he claims is the natural culmination of each human life, of history and of evolution. (One who doubts the relevance to psychological self-regulation of the mathematical notion of *closure* might here accuse Piaget of 'theorem-envy': is not mathematics even more misleading than physics as a theoretical model for psychology? We shall see that although Piaget himself was influenced by an overly narrow class of formalisms, rigorous accounts of psychological transformations are in principle possible.)

Even such a brief account of dialectic constructionism suggests the complexities of interpreting and evaluating Piaget's psychology and placing it in his thought as a whole. Fortunately, one is not faced with the added difficulty that would have been posed by drastic changes of opinion on his part. Piaget is not someone whose views have differed radically at different periods, like the 'early' and 'late' Wittgenstein. Nor is he like Freud, some of whose most famous ideas appeared many years after others. Naturally, Piaget's concepts have developed over his lifetime (their formalization usually increasing); and he has described himself as 'one of the chief revisionists of Piaget'. [H 703] But essentially his position has not changed.

However, the content and approach of Piaget's work have varied. After his youthful devotion to philosophical speculation and biology, he published in the 1920s several empirical studies of children's psychology, based largely on verbal interviews with children at the Jean-Jacques Rousseau Institute of Education in Geneva. [LTC; JRC; CCW; CCPC; MJC] These described, for example, children's socialization and growing ability to take another person's point of view; their use of language to argue and explain; their understanding of dreams, life, morality, and the origins of sun, water and trees; and their ideas about movement, force, mechanism and causality.

In 1925 Piaget's wife and co-worker Valentine Châtenay gave birth to Jacqueline, and the parents initiated a programme of detailed observation of the newborn baby (and, later, her siblings). The result was the theory of sensorimotor intelligence, published through the 1930s, which described the spontaneous development (well before the appearance of language) of a practical intelligence based in action, that forms and is formed by the infant's nascent concepts of permanent objects, space, time, number and cause. [OIC; CCR]

The next decade saw Piaget's account of growth into the pre-operational and operational stages, for which he studied children's active manipulation of experimental materials (beads, dolls' clothes, sticks, Plasticine, knots, levers, and so on) as well as their verbal behaviour. His experiments showed extraordinary ingenuity, in suggesting ways of 'externalizing' abstract and tacit thinking. In the 1940s he published (in some cases with Barbel Inhelder and Alina Szeminska) empirical studies of the growth of understanding of logic, number, mathematics, space, geometry, time, movement and symbolic thinking. [e.g. CCN; CCT; CCMS; CCS; CCG; PDI] These were more formalized in approach than the early 'naturalistic' reports of children's conversations, and in 1947 the first systematic theoretical statement of his psychology outlined a formal account of the developmental stages and the equilibratory structures of intelligence. [PI]

From the 1950s onwards, while continuing to publish empirical research (on thinking, perception, and memory), [e.g. GLT; EGL; MP; MI] Piaget has increasingly concentrated on theoretical and interdisciplinary writings inspired by his original aim of using psychology to integrate biology and epistemology. [e.g. IEG; LP; S; BK; IIP; GE; PGE; IDR] His Centre for Genetic Epistemology (founded in 1955) is explicitly interdisciplinary in character, attracting scholars not just of psychology but of the many fields Piaget sees as falling within the range of his theory.

The unusually broad scope of Piaget's theoretical writings results from his view that genetic epistemology deals with knowledge in general. Despite his claim to 'an encyclopaedic ignorance',[2] Piaget has held professorial appointments in philosophy, sociology and history of science as well as in psychology and education. He writes about the nature and history of logic, mathematics, cybernetics, physics, linguistics, semiology, anthropology and sociology as well as (and in relation to) the various branches of biology, philosophy and psychology. And he attempts an integrated epistemological account of these diverse fields wherein no one of them is strictly (or reductively) basic, since there is a 'circle of sciences' such that the laws of one science are based on those of another. Piaget is a polymath: one who knows about many different arts and sciences – but he is a synthesizing polymath, for whom many of the differences are more apparent than real.

Piaget's widely ranging discussions hold fascination and promise for readers who share his hankering for a single systematic theory of human knowledge. But his broad epistemological aims may seem irritatingly grandiose to those who prefer the detailed investigation of narrowly circumscribed topics (a style more characteristic of the Anglo-American than of the Continental intellectual tradition). And inevitably, despite his erudition, he makes mistakes.

Since many of his mistakes have a general significance in light of his overall system, the most appropriate response to them for our purposes is not to castigate nor even to correct so much as to understand them. For example, one should not merely say that in his theoretical formalizations of psychology he gets his mathematics wrong or uses logical concepts differently from logicians, nor simply puzzle over how his faulty mathematics might be patched up, but rather ask why he deformed logico-mathematical concepts in the way that he did. The answer (to be clarified in Chapter 7) is that he had available the formalisms only of algebra and logic with which to describe dynamic psychological processes of structural transformation, and had to deform them since algebra and logic – unlike some recent cybernetically based (computational) formalisms – are not well suited to the representation of dynamic self-regulating systems. Similarly, in his discussions of the practice and the history of mathematics, Piaget fails to realize the importance of proofs as opposed to structures in mathematics.[3] This relates to the same general weakness of Piagetian theory, its failure to specify *process* in intelligence.

For all his admirable stress on action as the context and

carrier of mental life, and for all his theoretical emphasis on the inner dynamics of equilibration (including an entire volume in 1975 devoted to different 'mechanisms' of equilibration [DT]), we shall see that Piaget's theory lacks specification of detailed procedural mechanisms competent to generate the phenomena it describes. (So, it should in fairness be said, do most other psychological theories.) This may seem surprising, not to say ironic, for Piaget's distinction lies in exhorting us to consider the dynamics of psychological development: the trouble is that his theoretical deformations of logic and algebra were not sufficiently different from their original 'non-dynamic' moulds.

It may be surprising also that the American Psychological Association did not choose to honour Piaget until his seventy-third year. For at thirty he was already famous in Europe; at forty he was given an honorary doctorate by Harvard University; and by mid-century his stature had increased still more. Yet the first comprehensive textbook in English that discussed his work and related it to American experimental psychology was not published until 1962.[4] Quite apart from the language barrier (not all his books were promptly translated), several features of his work tended to make it less acceptable to academic psychologists in America than to their European counterparts. Three of these still arouse much criticism; but the one of greatest historical importance has ceased to be an obstacle, because of independent developments within American psychology. The four features concerned are his prose style, his highly abstract theory, his methodology and his anti-behaviourist mentalism.

Piaget's prose style is hard to defend: he will win no prizes for clarity, brevity or wit. The quantity (and repetitiousness) of his prose is as daunting as its quality. He admits that he 'could not think without writing', [A 241] and he has already published nearly sixty books and hundreds of articles.

The abstract and systematic nature of his theory is off-putting to readers not used to his Continental style of thinking (and the obscurity and prolixity of his prose do not help). Correlatively, confident acceptance and fruitful criticism are each hindered since it is often hard to be sure just what claim he is making. Some critics object that his views are so vague as to be irrefutable. In particular, his systematizer's predilection for using identical theoretical terminology to characterize apparently distinct domains forces the query whether he is offering substantive unifying concepts (as he claims), fruitful metaphors or contentless verbiage.

For example, his terms 'equilibrium', 'assimilation' and 'accommodation' have clear meaning in the biological contexts from which they are drawn. But whether they are equally – or even usefully – clear in psychological or epistemological contexts (or in wider biological contexts, such as evolutionary theory and embryology) is controversial. So too is the question whether they offer explanations of cognitive growth, as opposed to polysyllabic descriptions of it – perhaps, but perhaps not, usefully identifying important phenomena requiring explanation in other terms. An American psychologist who deeply admires Piaget has dismissed his concept of equilibrium as 'surplus baggage', contributing nothing to theory or to experimental design save some 'confusing imagery' and serving merely to give Piaget 'a comforting sense of continuity with his early biological apprenticeship'.[5] Certainly, even highly abstract concepts like this can be scientifically useful: the abstract cybernetic concept of *feedback* (which Piaget sees as being very close to his notion of *equilibration*) has been fruitful in many different domains. But, if it is to be useful in various fields, an abstract systematizing concept (whether 'feedback', 'equilibration', 'structure' or any other) must be amenable to significantly parallel specifications at more detailed empirical levels. Many critics of Piaget argue that his theory does not adequately fulfil this requirement.

Piaget's methodology (especially in his earlier works) has often been criticized for its lack of statistics and controlled experimental design. He prefers a quasi-clinical method, in which individual children are questioned and observed in detail, to the statistically based comparison of large groups (although some of his later research uses statistical methods). This method originated in his early psychoanalytical interests and his studies of abnormal children at the Salpetrière hospital, [A 244] but even in his adolescent novel he said that science in general was overly 'quantitative' and should be more 'qualitative' in nature. [G 47]

He can now offer a philosophical justification of his methodology in structuralist terms. The structuralist's aim (whether he be Piaget, F. de Saussure, N. Chomsky, T. Parsons, or C. Lévi-Strauss) is not to make quantitative predictions based on statistical measures or correlational laws, but to express a formal system in terms of which 'the actual is now interpreted or explained as an instance of the possible' [S 38] (though many structuralists avoid questions about why *this* possibility was actualized rather than *that*, and *how*). Structuralists may therefore consider relatively few cases (fewer than a positivist philosophy of science would advise), but they typically believe that their theories are interesting because they mark universal – though highly abstract – features of the mind. Piaget is no exception: he is not like the true clinician, who is interested in *this* or *that* individual person, for he uses his 'clinical' method to study what he terms the 'epistemic subject', by which he means those aspects of the mind that are common to all individual subjects (at the same level of development). [S 139]

The sorts of criticism to which a structuralist theory is in principle open include objections that its concepts are not in fact universally applicable to all cases, objections that it does not unambiguously generate the fine structure of the theorist's specific observations, and objections (perhaps based on even more careful observations than the structuralist offers) that different theoretical interpretations can cover the same range of cases. Current criticisms, for instance, complain that Piagetian theory does not unambiguously predict his experimental observations, and also that Piaget often fails to design his experiments carefully enough to exclude non-Piagetian explanations. And before the comparatively recent rise of structuralism within psychology, American psychologists typically had little sympathy with Piaget's anti-positivist methodological approach.

They lacked sympathy also with Piaget's uncompromising mentalism, not to mention his habit of putting philosophical discussion in the forefront of his psychological writings. Until recently, American academic psychology has been strongly behaviourist in character, and positivist in philosophical tone. Behaviourists naturally rejected Piaget's humane insistence on defining psychology as the study of the *mind*, [6PS 114] and spurned his postulation of unseen mental schemata and operations underlying observable behaviour. And their positivist assumptions that empirical observation and empirically based theory can and should be sharply distinguished from mere philosophical speculation – as well as their eagerness to have psychology accepted as a *science* – caused them to react violently against the explicitly epistemological flavour of Piaget's work.

This disparaging attitude to Piaget's work is less common among psychologists today, largely because mainstream academic psychology is no longer behaviourist in nature. In particular, cognitive psychology (the study of thinking, language and intelligence) is markedly mentalistic, its theories positing inner processes, structures and representations within the mind that generate and guide intelligent behaviour and actively inform human thought and experience. Also (largely because of the influence of

Chomsky), current cognitive psychology is less strongly environmentalist than was behaviourism, more ready to concede that innate biologically based structures may have psychological importance. In these respects, one might say that psychology has caught up with Piaget.

This does not mean that all cognitive psychologists are Piagetians. Still less does it mean that they are Piagetians who believe that he has never been wrong about what children can or cannot do, or that he has never been vague about the (equilibratory) way in which they develop their intelligence. But there is an increasing readiness to turn to Piaget not just for his rich observational material but for his theoretical questions too. As we shall see, he raises many questions – and suggests controversial outline answers – that are currently engaging the attention of theoretical psychologists (and biologists) from outside as well as within the Piagetian tradition.

Many of his insights have entered into psychology as a whole, being so taken for granted that they are not thought of as specifically Piagetian (similar remarks apply to Freud). In some cases they are not *specifically* Piagetian, having entered mainstream psychology from other writers. For example, structuralist and nativist modes of explanation ousted behaviourist positivism with the work of Chomsky and (earlier) K. S. Lashley; and the mentalist explanation of behaviour in terms of inner schemata representing world and action in organized ways has been greatly influenced by the psychological views of F. C. Bartlett, K. J. W. Craik and M. L. Minsky. But Piaget was already recommending these sorts of psychological explanation in the 1920s (and, for biology, even before), though his brand of 'nativism' was more dialectical in nature than most later theories that likewise stressed innate, inherited principles.

So that the strengths of Piaget's work may be weighed against its weaknesses, I have tried in the following chapters not only to present his views but also to outline the main areas of criticism. Chapters 2 to 4 concentrate on his psychological experiments and theory, Chapter 5 deals with his philosophical interpretation of his psychology, and Chapter 6 puts his psychological theory into its biological context. In Chapter 7, which discusses the relevance to Piaget's psychological theory of his commitment to cybernetics, I argue that a recently developed approach to psychology (based on the attempt to provide machines with analogues of cognitive skills) can highlight and possibly remedy some deficiencies in Piaget's theory. In general, his account of the nature, preconditions, and results of the various mental transformations underlying cognitive achievements is too broadly sketched to express or properly to differentiate between them. This is true whether we consider his account of the baby's intelligence (the topic of Chapter 2), his description of the thought of the young child (presented in Chapter 3), or his views on mature logical reasoning (discussed in Chapter 4). Quite apart from empirical evidence suggesting the falsity of some of his factual claims, and from alternative theoretical interpretations of his experiments, one must take seriously the charge that he does not specify in sufficient detail precisely *how* the transformations he postulates are effected, or precisely *what* these transformations are. I shall suggest in Chapter 7 that computational concepts, with which he might be expected for various reasons to have a great deal of sympathy, are needed to express these matters precisely. Finally, in Chapter 8 I summarize the historical and continuing importance of Piaget's work.

For all the criticisms that can justly be made of him, there is no question but that Piaget is a modern master. At both observational and theoretical levels, his work has provided a stimulus to (or, more appropriately perhaps, a seed of) our understanding of the development of intelligence that is without equal. And the educational implications of his theory challenge many traditional views about what children should be doing (and how they should be doing it) in the classroom. It is no wonder that gallons of ink have been spilled in attempts to confirm or to refute his ideas. He still attracts both devoted disciples and castigating critics, who have little in common but a dogmatic insensitivity to the possibility that he may (like the rest of us) be sometimes right and sometimes wrong. Increasingly, however, cognitive and educational psychologists are aiming for a more balanced approach, wherein his pioneering observations and ideas are consolidated, elaborated, qualified and (where appropriate) rejected in the light of current psychological knowledge. This dialectical process of reconstruction of his theory is evidence of its intellectual vitality and developmental potential.

It is evidence, too, of the close relation between Piaget's psychology (wherein his greatest originality lies) and his biological and philosophical views. As if in confirmation of Piaget's belief that 'psychology, like all other sciences, can live and prosper only in an interdisciplinary atmosphere', [AP 651] current cognitive science (as we shall see) shows a growing interdisciplinarity. Increasingly, psychologists, biologists and epistemologists not only discuss each other's questions but find it fruitful to borrow – even if they have to adapt – each other's answers. Piaget expects no less of a healthy genetic epistemology.

2   The Intelligent Baby

For many people, babies are boring. And the more such people are interested in abstract intelligence or scientific knowledge, the more boring babies may appear to be. They cannot do much, it seems, and what they can do apparently bears little relation to the real stuff of human knowledge. Like kittens, they may be amusing; but they have little psychological and less epistemological significance.

Part of Piaget's achievement is to have shown how fundamentally mistaken this attitude is. He does not claim merely that an account of human knowledge should, for completeness's sake, include an understanding of how a baby learns the things that at birth she did not know. He claims that the basic organizing principles of logic and science start developing well before language. They are evident in and generated by the baby's sensory and motor actions, whose adaptive interactions with each other and with the environment become increasingly differentiated, co-ordinated and skilled. Abstract intellectual structures (such as class inclusion, order and reversibility) and basic epistemological concepts (such as space, object, cause and self) have clear beginnings in the practical intelligence of infants. This intelligence is mediated by the baby's sensory and motor systems, which she uses to change and learn from her environment in increasingly purposeful ways. And by adapting to her environment she creates her world, for a baby sucking is constructing a world of suckable things (not merely finding things in the world that she sucks).

Piaget sees successive psychological stages in the growth of intelligence, of which the first – the sensorimotor stage

– lasts from birth to about two years (all stage-ages are approximate and age has no theoretical importance). Piagetian stages and sub-stages mark differences in what children can do and cannot do. But he is not interested in specific performances (such as sucking, grasping or walking) so much as in the general principles of intelligence that organize the various performances and make them possible. He claims that a wide range of superficially distinct behaviours appear roughly simultaneously at each stage, because they are all generated by the same recently developed structure.

For instance, the sensorimotor stage or period is itself divided into six (sub-) stages. Illustrative examples will be given presently, but the stages are defined in abstract terms as follows: (1) reflexes and spontaneous movements – birth to one month; (2) the first repetitive habits, or primary circular reactions – one to four months; (3) actions to make interesting sights continue, or secondary circular reactions – four to ten months; (4) co-ordination of means and ends – ten to twelve months; (5) the discovery of means, or tertiary circular reactions – twelve to eighteen months; and (6) the beginning of representational thought, enabling the invention of new means by sudden comprehension – eighteen months to two years. (Stage 6 is transitional between true sensorimotor intelligence and pre-operational thinking.)

The significance of the stages for Piaget is that their order is invariant, because each one is an essential epistemological preparation for those that will follow. That is, each stage develops from, rather than merely adding to, the one before. So the point is not that at Stage 5 the baby can grasp (for example) for the first time: grasping is an innate reflex already present at Stage 1. The point is that she learns how to use her sensorimotor capacities in increasingly well-organized and differentiated ways, so that the grasping of Stage 5 is a very different matter from that of Stage 1.

Moreover, Stage 1 grasping does not lead to Stage 5 grasping by a simple linear sequence, whether unfolded by physiological maturation or triggered by environmental conditions. Rather, grasping develops in dialectical interaction with the child's environment, which itself is largely dependent on the developing constructive activities of the child. So although Piaget allows that bodily maturation and environmental (including social) pressures are important factors in cognitive development, their influence is dialectically mediated by the developing mind itself. This is why (as we shall see in Chapter 6) Piaget regards psychological development as essentially comparable with 'epigenesis' in biology.

The newborn baby shows spontaneous and reflex actions such as sucking, crying, grasping and moving the eyes, head, body or arms. But even reflexes are organized systems, whether viewed biologically or psychologically. They consist of interacting sensory and motor processes that manifest the same general structure on each occasion of use, as in the mutually adaptive actions of the flexor and extensor muscles at a joint. Some reflexes (such as sneezing to light) drop out, but others become more efficient as they are actively exercised by the baby. This observed differentiation of function, which continues throughout development, implies for Piaget that the underlying structure is increasingly differentiated also.

Piaget's rather cumbersome term for this spontaneous exercise of reflex (and, later, more complex) actions is 'reproductive, or functional, assimilation'. Through interaction with the environment, it involves a 'generalizing assimilation' (so that the baby starts to suck new objects, or even nothing at all) and a 'recognitive assimilation' (so that she learns to distinguish the nipple from other objects, and eventually suckable from non-suckable objects in general). As always, assimilation is accompanied by accommodation, and fairly early within the first months the baby learns how to move her head so as to find the nipple, and how to shape her mouth suitably to it.

Admittedly, reflex actions are often elicited by environmental stimuli (even a few minutes after birth, sucking is released by contact of the lips with the hands). And they are instigated also by bodily needs, such as hunger. But their spontaneous exercise is essential for their consolidation and development. So reflex development is largely autonomous, in that it results from the baby's inborn need to use and to generalize her psychological structures (a need Piaget compares with the body's need for the digestive assimilation of food).

Piaget sees this basic need for exercising one's capacities as continuing throughout life, in school and out of it, acting as the underlying dynamic of equilibratory cognitive improvements (spontaneous learning) at all intellectual levels. Whereas Freud and drive-reduction behaviourists alike see motivation in terms of an aim for quiescence, or release of tension, Piaget does not. He is comparable rather with those psychologists who posit motives of 'curiosity', or a need for 'competence' and who stress the importance of 'adaptation-levels' in motivation.[1] At all ages, the things that excite a child's curiosity and serve to extend her competence are 'neither what is too familiar . . . nor what is too new', [OIC 68] for the former provide no challenge because of surfeit, whereas the latter provide no challenge since they do not correspond to anything in her current structures and so cannot be assimilated (or accommodated to) by her.

The Stage 2 baby, accordingly, continues to exercise many of her reflexes and enlarges their scope. These are the reflexes that are elaborated into 'circular reactions'. Spontaneous movements of many kinds are repeated for their own sake (that is, for the sake of the bodily satisfaction they provide), and become increasingly smooth. For instance, thumb-sucking now appears as a habit. The Stage 1 baby, and even the baby in the womb, sometimes sucks her thumb; but she shows no tendency to repeat this action immediately for its own sake – if the thumb touches the mouth it is likely to be sucked, but that is all there is to it. Habitual thumb-sucking implies the ability to get the thumb into the mouth and, after removing it, to return to the same point of departure so as to repeat the spatio-temporal sequence all over again. In Piagetian terms, the sucking scheme has assimilated the thumb to itself and has accommodated itself to the thumb; moreover, the sucking, visual and arm-moving schemes have become to some extent co-ordinated in one stably organized structure, instead of functioning independently. A 'scheme' is the structure that is common to many actions in similar or analogous circumstances (a concept similar to F. C. Bartlett's 'schema'[2]). The baby's sensorimotor schemes are constructed out of perceptual and motor systems only; later, they will be integrated with symbolic and operational systems.

According to Piaget, the perceptual-motor co-ordination in the schemes of Stage 2 is very primitive. For instance, he says that early in Stage 2 the baby knows neither how to grasp what she sees nor how to bring what she grasps into her line of sight (she brings it to her mouth, not her eyes). But her looking and hand-moving schemes are now mutually adapted to a degree: when her hand happens to come within her sight it tends to stay there, and when her eyes happen to light upon her hand they tend to remain focused on it. Such behaviour is comparable to the way in which a simple cybernetic machine, governed only by direct feedback signals from its environment, maintains a steady state such as temperature. But as Piaget points out, it is not truly purposive or intentional (even though this type of stabilization is essential for purposive function). This is because the 'goal' or 'purpose' of the activity has to be directly perceived (as opposed to being anticipated or imagined), and because the 'goal' is attained relatively directly, without any series of intermediary actions hierarchically related as means to end. Piaget describes the gradual evolution of co-ordination between looking and grasping in terms of five (sub-sub-) stages. For instance, he claims there is a point at which the baby can grasp a seen object only if she can see her hand simultaneously with it; it is not (or not just) that she needs to see to guide her grasping hand, but rather that the idea (the co-ordinated scheme) of grasping-what-is-seen is activated only by the perceptual combination of hand and object. But soon, by the end of Stage 2, the baby can start reaching for a seen object even when her hand is hidden under her blanket. Piaget reminds us of W. Kohler's apes, who could join two sticks only if both were simultaneously in sight; but instead of the static structures posited by Gestalt psychology, Piaget stresses the development of increasingly well co-ordinated looking and grasping schemes.

It is in Stage 3 that we see the beginnings of intentional activity, and of what Piaget regards as 'intelligence' proper. In this stage, too, we see the initiation of interest in the external world for its own sake. The baby now employs sensorimotor procedures to make interesting sights last. That is, she repeats her actions (exercises her schemes) not just for the sake of doing them or for the bodily satisfaction they may bring, but for the environmental effect that they may have. This word 'effect', however, has to be cautiously interpreted here. The baby's grasping a hanging cord is followed or accompanied by her toy bells ringing, and she grasps over and over again. However, even though she can now grasp what she sees and could grasp the cord if she wanted to, she does not grasp *the cord*. One can say that, in a sense, she notices that grasping the cord makes her bells ring. But she does not have a clear idea of means-end relations or of material causality (which for a sensorimotor being must necessarily go together), and does not realize that moving the cord is an essential instrumental element in the bell-ringing process. She will even grasp (or grasp the cord) to make something happen on the far side of the room: in general, her scheme of causality is 'centred' on her own actions. This is why Piaget says that her primitive sense of causal connection is a 'magical' one, rather than that she is merely ignorant of specific causes (as an adult may be when switching on a radio).

Without the elaboration and mutual co-ordination of sensorimotor schemes that occurred in the first two stages (and which continues throughout the whole period) she could not have understood and reacted to the cord-bell situation even to this limited degree. That is, cord (or grasping) and bell are not functioning for her as atomistic 'stimulus' and 'response' fortuitously threaded on the same associative string. On the contrary, 'every newly established connection is integrated into an existing schematism . . . The organizing activity of the subject must be considered just as important as the connections inherent in the external stimuli, for the subject becomes aware of these connections only to the degree that he can assimilate them by means of his existing structures.' [PC 5] Adapting a Kantian remark, one may say that for Piaget structures without experience are empty, but experience without structures is blind.

Stage 3 actions are intentional only in a minimal sense, in that the baby deliberately seeks to repeat movements that were performed fortuitously, with the general aim of conserving an interesting situation. But it appears that the means (grasping) is not separately identified or differentiated from the end (bells ringing) except after the event of their connection. No new means are employed to bring about the end, because the means-end scheme is stereotyped and inflexible. The baby cannot dissociate means from end so as to regroup means and end in new purposive schemes. Insofar as one can speak of the baby's having a goal, Piaget says, her goal arises from a chance happening that arouses interest, and cannot be set ahead of time or followed in different ways.

True co-ordination of means and ends appears in Stage 4, wherein the goal is apparently conceived of independently from the instrumental acts that will be used as means. The baby's goals arise only in the context of perceived facts (so are not context-free states for which the baby reflectively formulates plans), but the baby tries out various known actions in the attempt to reach her goals. For instance, to get at a piece of paper on her pram-hood she may shake herself, then wave her arms, then pull a string on the pram while staring at the paper, and finally reach out for it. She can overcome obstacles in a purposeful way. For instance, she may move her mother's hand toward a toy that is out of reach, or she may lift the handkerchief that is hiding it.

This last activity implies that in some sense she 'knows' the toy is under the handkerchief even though she cannot see it. Before Stage 4, says Piaget, babies do not have a concept of permanently existing objects, with spatial relations (objectively) independent of their own actions. If a toy they are playing with is covered by a handkerchief they will either lose all interest or show distress without any attempt to grasp the handkerchief (though at the end of Stage 3 they will remove the cover if the toy is partly visible). Moreover, only very gradually do they learn to track an object through space as it is hidden first under a cushion, then a handkerchief, then another cushion. Even a Stage 4 child will look only under the first cushion, ignoring the other two places: the first cover seems to act as a sign of the presence of the object because of its earlier perceived association with it. And only in Stage 6 does the baby anticipate unseen movement reliably: before then, if her train passes behind a chair she will look for it to reappear at the point where it disappeared, instead of at the far side of the chair. Only by this stage, then, is the infant's scheme of space independent of her own actions and perceptions.

However, the Stage 4 infant's newly developed understanding of object permanence, spatial relations, and causality enables her (unlike the Stage 3 child) to apply known means to new ends in a broadly sensible way, rather than merely trying to repeat single, magical, means-end connections experienced by chance. That is to say, the underlying dissociation and flexible regrouping of schemes (involving primitive concepts of classes and relations such as cord, bells, pulling, grasping, here, there and between) allows for the generation of indefinitely many specific action-plans conforming to the same general purposive scheme. Clearly, this generative possibility posited by Piaget is essential for intelligent problem-solving (though to posit its existence is not to specify the detailed transformations involved, as we shall see).

The Stage 5 baby shows even greater curiosity, anticipation and purposive flexibility, which involve and in turn contribute to a better understanding of object permanence, causal relations and spatial displacements. New means are now discovered and even actively searched for 'experimentally', by trial-and-error differentiation of the means already known. True 'play' appears, in which the baby experiments in various ways with different objects, actively differentiating her sensorimotor schemes in doing so. If she is trying to reach a toy on a blanket, the baby may touch or pull the blanket; noticing that it moves, she then immediately pulls it firmly towards herself, with the intention of getting the toy. This implies, among other things, a complex understanding of what it is for one thing to be on top of another thing – an understanding which includes the knowledge that if the latter moves then the former moves in the same direction. Similarly, the baby who experiments with a stick outside her playpen in order to find a position in which she can bring it between the bars, or who (in her crawling or early walking) makes a detour around an obstacle so as to reach her goal, evinces an integration (or mutual co-ordination) of schemes expressing means-end relations with schemes embodying the structure of spatial displacements.

Piaget sees clear precursors of adult reasoning in Stages 4 and 5, largely because the 'mobility' or late sensorimotor schemes (their dissociations, regroupings and co-ordinations) gives them a general assimilatory power. For instance the relation of *order* (which will later be used in abstract operations of *seriation*) characterizes the temporal organization of means-end behaviour, since the blanket has to be grasped before it can be pulled, and pulled before the toy is reached – only then can the toy be grasped and sucked. Similarly, *class inclusion* is foreshadowed in the hierarchical differentiation of subschemes: a baby who knows that one way of moving something is to pull it, another to kick it, another to get her mother to pull it . . . is analogous to the child who knows that the class of beads includes the subclass of green beads. Non-Piagetian psychologists have recently suggested that the hierarchical classification of concepts is ultimately based in representations and inferential processes originally developed with regard to matters like the perception of spatial location.[3] Piaget, too, sees spatial relations as important foundations of logical thinking, the scheme of space as a precursor of logical or 'operatory' schemes. For example, he likens operational *reversibility* to the baby's practical knowledge that a toy may be successively put under this cushion or that one, and back again, and to her appreciation of the fact that the best way to reach a place may sometimes involve a detour during which one is travelling *away* from the goal-position. He likens mature *conservation* to the baby's concept of object-permanence, and he sees imitation and even repetition of actions as significantly analogous to logical *one : one correspondence*.

Logical thinking will develop out of these cognitive structures, which are themselves constructed by the baby's sensorimotor intelligence. But since this intelligence is not reflective, being closely tied to perceptual and bodily actions, it cannot make judgements in abstraction from the sensorimotor milieu. As Piaget puts it, 'the involvements between the schemata are not yet regulated by a system of internal norms : the only verification of which the child is capable is of the type of *success* and not of *truth*.' [OIC 240] The epistemological leap from practical success to the more abstract species of success which is truth is made possible by the development of 'systematic', or 'reflective', intelligence.

All intentional acts, for Piaget, are generated by 'empirical' or by 'systematic' intelligence. Empirical intelligence is shown in Stages 3 to 5, in which the baby's actions are 'controlled by things themselves and not by deduction alone'; systematic intelligence makes its appearance in Stage 6, wherein acts are controlled 'from within by the consciousness of relationships [and so mark] the beginning of deduction.' [OIC 150] Where Stages 4 and 5 showed the *co-ordination* and (empirical) *discovery* of means respectively, Stage 6 introduces the *invention* of new means by purely mental combinations. Piaget compares this to the 'insight' of the Gestalt psychologists, but unlike them insists that intelligent intuition requires the previous development of increasingly differentiated and mutually co-ordinated structures. For example, 'a child confronted by a slightly open matchbox containing a thimble first tries to open the box by physical groping (reaction of the fifth stage), but upon failing, he presents an altogether new reaction : he stops the action and attentively examines the situation (in the course of this he slowly opens and closes his mouth, or, as another subject did, his hand, as if in imitation of the result to be attained, that is, the enlargement of the opening), after which he suddenly slips his finger into the crack and thus succeeds in opening the box.' [PC 12] (In Chapter 7 we shall note that there are *diverse* ways in which opening the mouth might enter into the baby's attempt to open the box, and that Piaget does not specify precisely *how* it helps the child).

Piaget's term 'imitation' is crucial here. He interprets the baby's mouth or hand movements (which would not occur in an older child) as an imitative representation of the opening of the box. He claims that in a primitive sense, they symbolize the action which will eventually be performed on the box, apparently somehow substituting for them mentally in the internal representation and planning of intentional action. Motor imitation has occurred before this and, according to Piaget, develops in a characteristic fashion. He reports that even a Stage 2 baby will sometimes repeat her own action if an observer does the same thing immediately after she does; in Stage 3, the baby will imitate actions initiated by the observer, provided that she can already make those movements and that she can see herself making them; only in Stage 4 (says Piaget) is the baby able to mimic actions for which she does not already possess fully differentiated schemes, and only then can she imitate an action such as opening and shutting the mouth which she cannot see (as well as feel) herself doing. This ability to imitate without visual self-monitoring implies a relative freedom of the imitative scheme from current perception, but such imitation does not occur in purposeful problem-solving (nor in the absence of the person imitated) until Stage 6. Later, Piaget says, the child will be able to use internalized imagery or verbal thought, the external imitative movements being entirely suppressed or by-passed (though just how this 'use' is possible is not yet understood).

Stage 6 leads on to the intuitive thinking of the pre-operational child, which further develops the representational or 'semiotic' functions of the mind. These are symbolic functions such as gesture, role-playing, drawing, imagery and language, which are mediated by stable internalized representations of action that are independent of the here-and-now. An infant who represents an absent cat by miaowing or by miming the act of stroking it is somehow using an abbreviated form of her sensorimotor scheme by which she has constructed her understanding of cats. Her mental image of a cat (or of stroking one) is an internalized sign equally based in her cat-scheme, which becomes assimilated to (part of) that scheme. Finally, the word 'cat' comes to be assimilated to the same scheme and so can function as a spoken (or, later, silently thought) symbol of cats. Recent research has confirmed that pre-linguistic children (with vocabularies as small as fifteen words) can categorize and manually sort things on the basis of perceptual and functional attributes, and that their categorizations later support and are in turn objectively differentiated by their learning of the socially accepted classifications coded in language.[4] The inner psychological details of the semiotic functions are, however, still obscure.

Many cognitive psychologists use the term 'representation' in a wider sense than Piaget, according to which one might almost say that he has got things the wrong way round. Instead of saying that external actions become internalized in the mind, they would insist that inner actions (that is: transformations of representations) precede and control all bodily action.[5] Piaget admits that in the broad sense comprising 'all consciousness of meaning', [OIC 147] even the newborn baby's reflexes (and animal instincts) are representational – although he prefers to say that 'the baby forms and uses significations' [PC 52]; and in the correlatively broad sense of 'knowledge', all biological creatures are said by Piaget to embody knowledge. We shall see in Chapters 6 and 7 that some biologists and many psychologists discuss the 'representation of knowledge' in a way that conforms to Piaget's broader sense of these terms, which includes what he calls 'significations'. Normally, however, Piaget reserves the term 'representational' for thinking that is abstracted from (reflective of) immediate perception and action. Fully purposive action, as well as logical thinking, presupposes the construction of covert representations (internalized actions) by means of which the child's intelligence is largely freed from the specific situation. In this sense, and even though it involves the attribution of meanings, sensorimotor intelligence (Stages 1 to 5) does not involve representations, and does not qualify for Piaget as 'thinking'. (Piaget's terminology thus obscures the fact that goals are always 'imaginary' insofar as goal-states do not exist before being achieved.)

In its broad outlines, Piaget's pioneering account of the sensorimotor period (based on his own three children) has held up well on further investigation. To some extent, this is due to the fact that there is a necessary (as opposed to a contingent) relation of ordering between the stages. It is barely conceivable that Stage 5 should occur before Stage 1; if it did, the term 'regression' would seem almost as inappropriate as 'development', for we would have difficulty in interpreting it as a natural process. This is why Piaget is sometimes accused of offering us 'logical truths dressed up in psychological guise, such as that learning must proceed from the simple to the complex, or that concrete operations with objects must precede abstract thought about them.'[6] However, we shall see in Chapter 5 that Piaget questions the implicit assumptions that lie behind such accusations: namely that a sharp distinction can be drawn between philosophical and scientific approaches to epistemological questions, and that conceptual truths are always self-evident and fully recognized. (Even so, some critics charge Piaget with the opposite fault, saying that Piagetian stage-order is contingent on education, and that different methods of teaching might lead to a different ordering of stages.[7])

Piaget's account has endured also because his theoretical questions, about the course of differentiation and coordination of increasingly purposive schemes, involving epistemologically basic concepts such as space and cause, are an essential and imaginative preliminary to any adequate account of the processes of 'equilibration' in sensorimotor development. But no such account has yet been given, and in Chapter 7 we shall see that even Piaget's most recent attempts to characterize sensorimotor equilibration are insufficiently precise.

Two general (and connected) criticisms may be made, each of which should be borne in mind in the following chapters because they apply also to his accounts of behaviour in older children. First, he tends to overestimate the unity and distinctness of the stages. Admittedly, he constantly gives examples of 'stage-anomalous' behaviour, and warns against assuming that the stages are either neatly homogeneous or sharply separated. But his own, and later, observations suggest that the concept of *stage* is less appropriate than he believes, for it unavoidably implies a fairly sudden and extended qualitative change.

Second, Piaget tends to underestimate the complexity of children's cognitive achievements. And he does this in two senses: he tends to underestimate the competence of children at a given age, whereas the evidence sometimes suggests that even younger children may be able to do things he sees as typical of that age; and (this will be clarified in the discussion of computational concepts in Chapter 7) he tends to be unaware of the large variety of subtly different psychological processes that might contribute to a given achievement – such as the previously cited example of a baby's opening a box to get the toy inside it. Both these criticisms, however, should be set against the fact that for many years it was Piaget himself who was outstanding in pointing out some of the structural complexity of behaviour that others might see as relatively simple skills, describable in stimulus-response terms. Tying shoelaces intelligently, for example, depends on development of the topological aspects of the scheme of space, so that the child who understands knots has not merely been trained to execute a series of successive movements. [CCS] And at the sensorimotor level, Piaget pointed out some of the often unsuspected complexity of grasping (even in Stage 1, never mind Stage 5), or of looking. This remains true even though recent attempts to make hand-eye machines show the complexity of these activities to be significantly greater than even Piaget allows.

Examples of the first sense in which Piaget underestimates children's achievements include 'egocentrism', to be discussed in Chapter 3. Another is his claim that prior to sensorimotor Stage 3, babies cannot exercise their motor schemes so as to make interesting sights continue. Recent work on operant conditioning in very young babies shows that Stage 1 or Stage 2 babies can be experimentally induced to suck (for example) when given the reward of seeing an interesting pattern. Some workers have even suggested that the looking, hearing and grasping schemes are innately co-ordinated and very soon integrated to a much greater degree than Piaget claims, and accordingly that the object-concept (or various object-properties on which it is based) is a much earlier achievement than he says. For instance, babies of thirty days old have been reported to show distress when hearing their mother's voice (through a loudspeaker) coming from a point greatly displaced from the place where they can see her sitting. And it has been claimed that babies of only a few days old can reach for and grasp objects *and* show distress on 'touching' empty air (having been experimentally induced to reach for a visual illusion); even stranger, they have been reported to reach for an illusory 'thick' rod with thumb and fingers more widely separated than when reaching for a 'thin' rod.[8]

Some of these strikingly anti-Piagetian claims have not been replicated by other workers, and there are methodological flaws in many of the experiments.[9] Nevertheless, there is increasing evidence that the newborn baby's perceptual system is already (innately) equipped to *discover* various environmental features which according to him have to be gradually *constructed* by way of the baby's instrumental activities.[10] Such features include invariants such as object-permanence, depth and other (non-metric) spatial relations. Perception, accordingly, is now thought to be a more active, competent process (even in the newborn) than Piaget believes – though this is not to deny that the baby's instrumental actions are very important in enabling her to construct the external world of objects with specific properties and functional potential. In addition, recent studies suggest a greater degree of organization of innate reflexes (motor and perceptual) than Piaget described. In terms of his dialectical distinction between rationalist and empiricist epistemologies (to be discussed in Chapter 5), this is to say that the human mind is rather more 'rationalist' in nature than he allows. But one should not forget that it is largely Piaget's theory that has led to these experimental investigations: current developmental psychology would be very different without him and, surely, considerably poorer.

A final question relates to the way in which one should interpret Piaget's view that sensorimotor experience is a necessary preliminary in the development of intelligence. Normal sensorimotor experience involves active manipulation (based on the grasping scheme) and active locomotion (based on the scrawling scheme). But a middle-aged woman born without any functional use of her limbs nevertheless has normal logico-mathematical intelligence (one might say 'above normal', since she helps her friends complete tax-forms). Though her head is normal for her age, her body 'was that of a neonate – albeit about two or three times the size of a month-old infant. Her arms and hands were "absolutely" infantile. They stuck out from her body exactly as an infant's do, moving occasionally but showing no purpose whatsoever.'[11] And a child born without limbs or digits was found at three to have normal sensorimotor intelligence, with a corresponding concept of object permanence (although as a baby he had learned to bat and roll objects with his head and trunk, and from the age of two-and-a-half he used a simple hooked prosthesis attached to his shoulder).[12]

Both these individuals could control their mouths, move their eyes, and turn their heads and trunks at will, so they were not totally devoid of sensorimotor schemes that might form the basis of intelligent co-ordinations. Piaget himself has said that he does not see such cases as contradicting his theory.[13] He claims merely that sensorimotor experience *of some sort* (which normally involves manipulation and locomotion) is essential for the growth of knowledge: 'sensorimotor activity has to be taken in a very general sense, and does not necessarily imply moving your hands, running around, etc. . . . It implies that activities are assimilated and accommodated, and this is the case with any child that lives, since it has to eat and drink (involving assimilation and accommodation – one drinks and eats very different things, and adjusts the movements according to the substance), and since it has perceptual activity (movements of the eyes and the head, if that is possible) also follows the same patterns of co-ordination.'[14] However, the issue remains somewhat equivocal, and in my view highly embarrassing for Piagetians since so many of his examples rest on the assumption of sensitive feedback from finely discriminated limb and digit movements; this type of feedback is not available to the limbless child, even if he can voluntarily bat and roll objects with his head or body. The way in which schemes of space, time, cause and hierarchical goal-directed action develop in very deprived children (such as thalidomide babies) is still highly unclear, and the more one stresses *construction* as opposed to *discovery* in cognitive development, the more problematic such cases appear.

But the fact that even grossly handicapped babies may achieve normal intelligence seems to endorse Piaget's stress on the autonomous development of knowledge, as opposed to its passive determination by experience. Similarly, although recent ingenious and technically sophisticated experimental studies of the first weeks of life show young babies to be able to do even more than Piaget's home-based observations suggested, they fully endorse his claim that babies are born already possessing structures with which to organize their experience (and so underscore the inadequacy of William James's famous description of the newborn's mind as 'a blooming, buzzing confusion'). Our biological endowment of intellectually relevant structures is apparently rich and flexible enough to enable human intelligence to mature even without the manipulative experiences that are so important to the normal baby.

3 The Intuitive Child

The infantile language, uncertain motor co-ordination and unsocialized behaviour of two- or three-year-olds remind us that they are not miniature adults (though in some cultures they have been treated as such).

But children between four and seven may seem very like adults, albeit ignorant ones. They are relatively socialized, apparently having learnt that consideration of other people's interests and observance of moral rules are expected of them by adults and their peers. Not only are they articulate, but they appear to reason abstractly using words like *same*, *more*, *sort of*, *how*, *why* and *because*. At school, they have mastered reading, writing and simple arithmetic. The first two of these skills ostensibly enable them to take in and express new knowledge (hence the traditional importance of verbal skills in education), while the third seemingly demonstrates a logical reasoning power shared with their parents. With even better teaching, it seems, they could achieve this power much earlier.

Piaget claims that the assumptions behind this view are questionable, and in many cases false. Even a seven-year-old is not a mini-adult, if this means that she has essentially the same sorts of knowledge and thinking processes as the adult but (because of her briefer experience) fewer known facts or learnt behaviours. Her understanding of the moral and material world is still largely subjective or self-centred, and her grasp of mathematical and causal reasoning is inadequate even in apparently simple problems because she has not yet developed 'operational' structures (of classification, seriation and reversibility) which generate a truly logical understanding. In sum, many of the ways in which her knowledge differs from her mother's are due not to mere ignorance, but to structural features that characterize pre-operational intelligence as a whole.

These features have to be constructed by the 'intuitive' or 'conceptual' thought of the four-to-seven-year-old before they can be reconstructed on the operational level in late childhood and adolescence. This series of successive reconstructions (like their sensorimotor precursors) takes time, and can be educationally or culturally accelerated only within limits. Piaget says he is not interested in 'the American question' of what these limits are, and how education might speed up stage-development, so much as in the fact that the order of stages is invariant since each one is a reconstruction of its predecessor. He admits that cross-cultural research shows Western (urban) education to be an accelerating factor in the development of operational intelligence (even though Piagetian assessments of intelligence are less affected by this factor than are standard psychometric intelligence tests). [NS] But he predicts (what has by and large been confirmed[1]) that the progression of stages will be broadly comparable in all cultures, with or without formal schooling and whether based on hunting or on agriculture. And he disagrees with educationalists such as J. S. Bruner, who claims that 'any idea or problem or body of knowledge can be presented in a form simple enough so that any particular learner can understand it in a recognizable form.'[2] 'Intellectual growth contains its own rhythm,' says Piaget, and 'speeding up cannot be indefinitely continued.' [BK 21]

Educational methods should take account of the structured nature and self-regulated development of intelligence. Piaget's concept of intrinsically motivated exercise (functional assimilation) applies to the schoolchild no less than to the baby. It implies that children are not naturally motivated primarily by external rewards or Skinnerian 'reinforcements' (excessive use of which in schools may warp their spontaneous development), and it implies also that each child will develop gradually at her own rate, having a natural tendency to differentiate her intellectual powers but little interest in learning strings of unstructured – and so largely unintelligible – facts. Premature teaching may be worse than useless since it may mask radical incomprehension by a spurious 'understanding' and so divert both teacher and child from the imminent structural developments that should be claiming their attention.

In the pre-operational stage, dialectical interaction with the external environment is still important for the development of intelligence. So too is the still increasing bodily co-ordination of the child, for the sensorimotor schemes concerned in body-control will act as the structural base for more obviously 'intellectual' achievements. This is why Piagetian educationalists ensure that children of two to four and four to seven, attending nursery and primary schools respectively, are encouraged to experience diverse materials and helped to discover – or, more accurately, to construct – their conceptualizable properties for themselves. For this reason, too, Piagetians favour physical activities (such as threading beads, tying knots, dancing) that develop the child's general understanding of space and time as well as her finely discriminatory movements.[3]

Piagetians criticize excessive stress on reading and writing in primary schools, believing that it may hinder the spontaneous growth of intelligence.[4] Premature teaching is often heavily reliant on the linguistic responses of the child. It is misleading because the child's understanding of words changes through time. According to Piaget, spoken language does not bring with it a mature rational intelligence: it assists but is distinct from logic. And the second-order linguistic skills of reading and writing are even less relevant to the young child's intellectual development. He cites evidence suggesting that the growth of logical thinking is much less delayed in deaf-and-dumb children (whose linguistic deficit is enormous) than it is in children blind from birth, who cannot make the wide range of sensorimotor co-ordinations that are naturally made by the sighted.[5] (Some more recent evidence indicates that blind children are not delayed in their logical development, so the question remains open.[6])

Piaget insists that before understanding can be internalized linguistically it must exist in a practical form. Indeed, Piagetians see the baby's sensorimotor action patterns as essential developmental conditions for the acquisition of syntax – and criticize Chomsky's stress on the 'innateness' of grammatical structures accordingly (though they do not deny that structures inherited from our evolutionary precursors must underlie both language and sensorimotor intelligence).[7] Just as sensorimotor co-ordinations provide the structural seeds of logic, so they allow for the development of abstract linguistic relations such as word-order, noun and verb, subject and object, and recursively embedded phrases: it is because the Stage 5 baby has developed many-levelled goal-hierarchies that she has the structural basis for assimilating sentences like 'Put the teddy *with the brown eyes* on the table.' And these primitive sensorimotor co-ordinations are further developed by practical action in the pre-operational stage.

It follows that activities such as dressing dolls (large hats for large dolls) and laying tables (one knife for each plate) are more important for intellectual development than is learning to spell or to recite the multiplication tables. A young child who says 'Two twos are four,' or who does the sum in figures, does not yet know (understand) what her teacher knows about cardinal numbers or the equivalence of sets. It is not just that she (like many adults) has never heard these technical terms: she does not yet have even an unspoken, or practical, understanding of such matters. She has to discover or construct for herself the realization that two dolls need two hats, two walking sticks, two plates . . . And she has yet to construct the scheme basic to ordinal number, which ensures that it is the medium-sized doll who gets the medium-sized stick and hat. Similarly, if her teachers have been misguided enough to teach her to parrot the list of recent British monarchs, she will not thereby have achieved the understanding that George III came before George IV in time.

The relevant intellectual structures' are developed through her own activities of comparing, ordering and sorting physical objects and bodily actions. So a child whom the traditionalist might see as 'just playing with beads' is spontaneously developing abstract structures such as the schemes of seriation and classification, which in their later operational form will organize logico-mathematical thinking in general. While beads and dolls' clothes are not important, their educational function is (especially with the help of a sensitive teacher, who can guide the child's attention to structurally significant aspects of the 'play' situation).

As we shall see, Piaget claims that practical as well as verbal observations show that a pre-operational child's understanding of terms like *all*, *some*, *sort of*, *equals* and the like is systematically different from that of a nine- or twelve-year-old. Similarly, a child who says the sun is alive is not just ignorant, as the adult would be who said that coal is an inorganic rock. Her current concept of 'life' is itself different from the adult's (though this is not to say that there is a unique adult concept of 'life'), and only careful and extended questioning can diagnose her understanding of it. In general, since intelligent creatures construct their own meanings, rather than passively picking them up from the world (including books and teachers' remarks), one cannot assume that a word (or a mathematical sign, such as '2' or ' – ') used by a child expresses the same meaning as it does when used by another child of the same age or by an adult. So Piagetians criticize intelligence tests or standardized pupil assessments which depend superficially on the verbal responses (and the sums) of the child instead of exploring the idiosyncratic structure of her active understanding of the concepts expressed by her words (or mathematical signs).

The words used by two- to four-year-olds, says Piaget, do not express what he calls 'concepts' at all, but rather 'pre-concepts'. These are 'the notions which the child attaches to the first verbal signs', and they 'remain midway between the generality of the concept and the individuality of the elements composing it', [PI 128] so that no conceptual distinction appears to be made between *slug* and *slugs*, even though both these verbal signs are used by the child. Piaget sees this not as a mere ignorance of grammar, but as a lack of the conceptual structures embodying the relations of *all* and *some* that are part of any truly conceptual scheme. So he says that the pre-conceptual scheme 'is not yet a logical concept and is still partly something of a pattern of action and of sensori-motor assimilation.' [PI 128]

Even the second pre-operational period (the 'conceptual' or 'intuitive' stage, from four to seven) shows thought that apparently cannot handle class-inclusion problems involving explicit reference to logical relations such as *all*, *some* and *more*. The school-age child may say, for example, that there are more black cows than cows (although in Chapter 7 we shall see that slight verbal changes in questioning may give strikingly different results). Similarly, up to about seven years a child may insist on seemingly contradictory statements about beads in a box: she admits that the beads are all wooden, and that if all the wooden ones were taken away then no beads would remain in the box; and she sees both that there are more brown beads than white ones and that some white ones would remain if the brown beads were removed; nevertheless, she repeatedly insists that there are more brown beads than wooden ones, 'because there are only two or three white ones'. And if asked to imagine what would happen if she made a necklace either with the wooden or with the brown beads, she will sometimes say, 'If I make a necklace with the brown ones, I could not make another necklace with the same beads, and the necklace made of wooden beads would have only white ones.' [PI 133]

In general, intuitive thought (and action) involves glaring contradictions – or what will later seem so to the same child – that are not recognized as such by the pre-operational intelligence. (Adults contradict themselves too, of course, but rarely in such an 'obvious' way.) As well as saying there are more black cows than cows, or more brown beads than wooden ones, the young child may say that her sister doesn't have a sister. (And, as we shall see in Chapter 4, she may be quite incapable of putting dolls in order of height, or aligning blocks into a staircase.) So to Alice's cry that 'One can't believe impossible things,' a Piagetian might reply that one can – provided one cannot understand that they are impossible.

However, the main thrust of Piaget's work is not to make essentially negative points about what children cannot do, or about their failure to reject the impossible. Rather, it is to persuade us what a great, and largely autonomous or untaught, achievement it is to come to recognize (and to construct the limits of) the possible. The White Queen proudly assured Alice that she could believe 'as many as six impossible things before breakfast'. But she had nothing to say about either how she managed this or how, after breakfast, she came to realize the impossibility of the things she had earlier believed. Piaget, by contrast, offers a developmental theory specifically intended to show how the intellectual construction of the possible begins in the sensorimotor structures of babies' intelligence, continues throughout the intuitive stage, and reaches its zenith in the abstract logical structures of formal operational knowledge. We should picture this progression not as the passage from an absence of understanding to its presence, but as the evolution of a superior, better-differentiated form out of a more lowly one. Just as the newborn's inefficient grasping is real grasping, and a worm is a real, though lowly, living creature, so – says Piaget – pre-operational thinking 'is in no way irrational', despite its logical immaturity. [PI 133] (Perhaps one should say rather that it is not *non*-rational, for Piaget does believe operational thought to be superior in rationality.)

This logical immaturity consists in a tendency to think in terms of imagined actions that are represented (or actual actions that are regulated) in ways analogous to perception rather than to operational thought. Piaget sees a gradual progression from 'simple' to 'articulated' intuitions, as relatively rigid perceptual regulations give way to more flexible quasi-operational or logical structures in the planning and monitoring of action. But even at the end of this stage, says Piaget, the child cannot consider several aspects of a situation or action-scheme all at once, and so cannot take advantage of the reversibility of many actions in order to understand the conservation of abstract intellectual structures such as number, substance or volume.

For instance, the child knows that brown and white beads can be separated and recombined indefinitely; and that water can be poured from a low fat jar into a tall thin one and back again (reaching the same level in the fat jar as before); and that a Plasticine snake can be transformed into a ball and thence to a snake again. But she cannot integrate these reciprocal intuitions so as to understand that since the wooden beads comprise all and only the brown and white ones there must be more wooden beads than brown ones, or that the amount of water or Plasticine remains constant despite transformations in its perceptual properties.

The child of four or five almost seems unable to recognize both that the snake gets thinner and that it gets longer: she will persist in saying either 'there's more Plasticine now' or 'there's less Plasticine', justifying her answers respectively by saying 'it's longer' or 'it's thinner'. By five or six she will pay attention to both these aspects, but not simultaneously: she will alternate between 'there's more' and 'there's less', alternating likewise between pointing out that 'it's longer now' and 'it's thinner now'. But she will not do what the older (concrete operational) child will do, namely co-ordinate these two perceptually based judgements so as to realize that they exactly compensate for each other at all times. So Piaget attributes her inability to understand (construct) conservation of substance to her failure to abstract from and co-ordinate her perceptually based intuitions. (Even these are intellectual *constructions*, according to Piaget, as opposed to purely sensory data by which the child *discovers* the properties of objects: 'Position in space, dimensions, solidity and resistance, colour in different lights, etc. . . . although perceived in the object itself, presuppose an extremely complex intellectual elaboration . . . In order to perceive these individual realities [different views of mountains, inkwells, or Plasticine snakes] as real objects it is essential to complete what one sees by what one knows.' [OIC 190])

Similarly, a pre-operational child has a shaky grasp of one-to-one correspondence and so an immature understanding of number. If a child of four or five is shown a line of red sweets and asked to put out as many yellow sweets as there are red ones, she will use a 'simple' intuitive judgement of perceptual correspondence between the ends of the two lines to regulate her actions. So her line will be equal in length but unequal in number, for she does not construct a line in which the yellow sweets correspond one-to-one with the red. The six- to seven-year-old will use a more 'articulated' intuition to regulate her setting out of the line, thus constructing a matching row of yellow sweets, one-for-one. But if one row is then 'stretched'. while she is watching, she will insist that the longer row has more sweets than the other (much as the same child is seduced by the perceived height of the water-level into saying that the thin jar has more water in it). At best, she will be doubtful about the numerical equivalence of the two rows, and may resort to actual counting to establish it experimentally.

This empirical correlate of abstract mathematical reasoning is crucial. For Piaget, the fact that we are born into a world in which we can count and recount, move and remove, combine and separate things over and over again, such that there is always some way of arriving at the same number, is an essential epistemological prerequisite of logic. Creatures living in a world of coalescing mercury droplets simply could not become scientists or mathematicians – unless they had countable, identity-preserving hairs, perhaps. And immobile, limbless creatures (including plants, most of whose 'movements' are irreversible growth) are also incapable of logical reasoning, since they have no sensorimotor experience enabling them to develop a scheme of space representing the fact that one can always moves one's body (or movable limbs) in indefinitely various ways so as to arrive at the same *place* (cf. the same *goal*, the same *number*, the same *state*). The structural features of space and object-identity which are learnt by the exploring baby somehow provide the organizational basis of the schoolchild's more abstract, logical, schemes (though just how this can be is not explained in detail by Piaget). His theory is a form of 'localism', which sees spatial relations as basic to semantics and so to all language and reasoning; recent work by non-Piagetian psychologists, linguists and philosophers makes localistic claims that have much in common with Piaget's approach.[8]

For Piaget, then, logic presupposes both 'given' facts of environment and biological embodiment, and 'autonomous' activity in the self-regulated exercise of biologically based capacities. The operational schemes of reversibility, conservation, class-inclusion and seriation develop only as the child comes to appreciate the abstract logical features of her own actions and intellectual constructions. Thus while it is an empirical fact that we are surrounded by countable, identity-preserving things, not by mercury droplets, it is we who must actively count them (which presupposes our actively constructing notions of identity and object-permanence in the sensorimotor stage), and we who must come to realize that our number concepts, like our concepts of substance or volume, can be so structured as to allow for reliable judgements of conservation. Given this interaction with the environment, pre-operational thought evolves autonomously to a more mobile and differentiated (articulated) level, until finally it gives rise to truly operational knowledge.

The evolutionary dynamic Piaget postulates is a series of equilibrations whereby the child's intellectual structures are reconstructed (not just reformulated or extended) at each stage, her 'egocentrism' giving way to objectivity by successive 'decentrations'. As he puts it:

> The structures of intelligence have to be entirely re-built before they can be completed; knowing how to reverse an object [as a baby can reverse her bottle] does not imply that one can represent a series of rotations in thought . . . Thought, springing from action, is indeed egocentric at first for exactly the same reasons as sensorimotor intelligence is at first centred on the particular perceptions or movements from which it arises. The construction of transitive, associative, and reversible operations will thus involve a conversion of this initial egocentricity into a system of relations and classes that are decentralized with respect to the self, and [the child's] intellectual decentralization (not to mention the social aspect) will in fact occupy the whole of early childhood. [PI 122-3]

The egocentrism of the pre-operational child is therefore not selfishness or inconsiderateness – even when it manifests itself in anti-social behaviour (as opposed to 'impossible' answers to questions) – for these imply the failure to take account of others' interests, knowing that they may differ from one's own. But Piaget claims that the young child has not yet constructed the set of organized meanings that would enable her (objectively) to realize that each self, including her own, is a centre of subjectivity with differing interests and beliefs. For example, the four-year-old concentrating ('centring') on the *length* of the Plasticine snake simply does not see that it could be viewed as *thin*; and the six-year-old, who sees it as thin as well as long, does not co-ordinate these viewpoints objectively so as to understand that the amount of Plasticine remains constant irrespective of its shape. Piaget describes the growth of objectivity as 'a kind of Copernican revolution' [PC 13] whereby the child's knowledge is progressively decentred, so that the ego (and its current perceptual experience) is no longer taken as the focus and origin of truth.

Piaget cites many observations in support of his claim that egocentrism is a pervasive feature of two- to seven-year-old thinking. For example, in his early work he found that young children interpret moral and other rules in a rigidly realist and result-focused manner. [MJC] They do not realize that the rules of marbles, say, are not God-given and could be altered by general agreement; nor can they accept that a child who accidentally breaks ten plates while helping her mother is less 'naughty' than one who breaks only two while stealing the jam. In his early work also, he claimed that almost half the speech of very young children is egocentric speech, spoken monologue (whether individual or collective in nature) that does not – and often is not even intended to – communicate with others. [LTC] Even at six, a child will assume that her interlocutor knows everything that she does, so will not explain pronouns or fill in background details. Again, a four- or five-year-old will say that she has a sister, but that her sister has none. This implies, says Piaget, a general inability to take another person's point of view. And Piaget has studied children's ability to take another's 'point of view' in a literal sense, saying that even seven- or eight-year-olds are unable to do this effectively. [CCS] The experiments he cites in this regard present a child with a toy landscape including mountains, houses and so on, in which a doll is placed looking in a direction different from the child's line of sight. The child is then asked either to describe what the doll sees or to pick that one out of a set of pictures which shows what the doll sees. Even eight-year-olds often fail, and younger children are very likely to describe the scene (or choose the picture) as they see it themselves.

Piaget believes that the ability to decentre develops out of the child's experience of walking round and handling things, which are then seen from different points of view, and also out of her arguments and negotiations with adults and with other, similarly egocentric, children. The educational implication is that primary schools should encourage co-operation and talking, as well as manipulative play, not purely for the social skills that these activities will develop but for their importance in developing objectivity or intellectual decentring in general.

Piaget's claims about egocentrism have not gone unchallenged, and it seems that, although he has identified an important aspect of thinking that is especially prominent in young children (because they are so reliant on perception, which necessarily involves a point of view), he underestimates the extent to which even infants can put themselves in another's place. This is to say that he underestimates the complexity of the co-ordinations between mental structures of which young children are capable.

For instance, children who cannot visualize the spatial relations seen by the doll in the mountainous landscape can tell where a child should place herself (in relation to several intersecting walls and several policemen) so as to be hidden from the policemen. Even three-year-olds achieve sixty-per-cent success, and four-year-olds get it ninety-per-cent right.[9] There are three ways in which this task differs from the landscape-task. First, the subject merely has to be able to answer a *yes-no* question about each policeman (Can the policeman see the child?), and does not have to decide precisely what view of the overall spatial scene the policeman has. Second, the task-situation can engage the child's interest in terms of her own experience: she, too, has tried to hide from people, especially after being naughty; but even many adults take little interest in landscapes. Last, and probably closely connected with the previous point, the child can easily make sense of the policeman-task; other experiments show that if exceptional care is taken to make sure that the child understands what she is required to do, even the landscape-task can be successfully tackled by many pre-school children.[10]

As for egocentrism in language, and the consequent lack of communicative competence and intent which Piaget attributes to young children, recent work suggests that the intent to communicate informs many of the child's actions even in the sensorimotor stage. For instance, J. S. Bruner's work on 'the ontogenesis of speech-acts' – or learning how to do things with words – applies the philosophical concept of speech-acts (requesting, seeking or giving information, thanking and so on) to the developing gestural and linguistic interactions between mother and child: what *people* mean is epistemologically prior to what *words* mean.[11] L. S. Vygotsky stressed the social functions of early speech, claiming that only gradually does outer speech become internalized as inner thought which can be used by the child in controlling her own actions; self-control, on this view, develops out of the acceptance of (linguistically expressed) control by others.[12] Finally, pre-operational children can and do alter their speech so as to take account of others' ignorance if they are convinced of that ignorance. So they will give background facts and avoid unexplained pronouns when talking to a younger child, or 'helping' a toy elephant who 'cannot see' or an adult holding her hands over her eyes. (Significantly, the more artificial situation of communicating with a *blindfolded* adult tends not to elicit appropriate communications from the child.)

Admittedly, young children may fail to realize the exact extent of the other person's ignorance (as adults often do), and so fail to communicate effectively. But Piaget's claim that they are in principle incapable of decentring, because they lack the organizational intellectual structures required to co-ordinate two points of view, clearly needs qualification. Complex co-ordinations such as would be needed for perfect performance in the landscape-task may well be impossible for structural reasons, not just because of the child's innocence of detailed facts. But psychologists will have to distinguish nicely between subtly different types of structural complexity, if the developing co-ordinations of which the child is capable are to be specified more precisely than they are in Piaget's theory.

Much current work in developmental psychology is aimed at this end, some of which uses the (cybernetically based) cognitive concepts that will be discussed in Chapter 7. One of the methodological problems is to decide when a child's failure is due to a lack of Piagetian structures or general principles of thinking, and when it is due to other factors (such as ignorance, incomprehension or short memory-span).[13] Some of these problems would arise in the interpretation of experimental results with respect to meticulously clearly expressed theories; but Piaget's relative obscurity, and his variability over different texts, do not help matters.

For example, P. Bryant has carried out a carefully planned series of experiments designed to show that preoperational children *can* make deductive transitive inferences and *can* use an external frame of reference to co-ordinate separate perceptual experiences.[14] Piaget claims (to the contrary) that the largely perceptual intuitions of

the young child are incapable of mediating such inferences, which arise (he says) only after the development of
the abstract logical structures of operational thought.
While agreeing with Piaget that perceptual processes and
strictly logical inferences must be distinguished, Bryant
even goes so far as to say, with respect to deductive inference and the use of external frameworks, 'where there
are developmental changes, they are the opposite of those
suggested by Piaget.'[15] Bryant claims that three- or four-
year-olds rely very strongly on perceptual framework cues
to make inferences, and have already started to abandon
these external cues in favour of more flexible strategies
by the time they are six. Space forbids discussion of the
details of Bryant's experiments here, or of Piaget's distinction between 'perception' and 'intelligence'. [MP] The point
of general methodological interest is that Bryant accuses
Piaget of not planning or controlling his experiments or
observations carefully enough to exclude alternative interpretations of his results. The results which Piaget takes to
show the child's inability to make transitive inferences are
interpreted by Bryant as being due to lack of understanding or shortness of memory-span on the child's part. According to Bryant, the child may have all the psychological
capacities relevant to making an inference but may be
unable to assemble them in the way needed to succeed.

Significantly, Bryant claims that *many* features of young
children's understanding (including their grasp of number
as well as their perceptual judgements) are generated by
transitive inferences relative to an external standard. He
does not merely cite one case of such an inference, in
the belief that this would suffice to contradict Piaget. In
general, when assessing the power of criticisms of Piaget
that are based on the investigation of specific task-situa-
tions, one should remember that Piaget's theoretical concern is the whole intellectual system. Piaget's structuralist
approach seeks to integrate the entire range of psychological phenomena coexisting at a given stage, showing

them to be essentially comparable. Passing from one stage to another, it is the broadly similar (and interrelated) development of the schemes of space, time, order, identity, cause . . . that interests him. And as regards fully operational thinking, it is the co-ordinated employment of these concepts in their abstract or scientific forms with which he is concerned. Piecemeal 'refutations' of Piaget thus have to be interpreted with caution.

Piaget's account of the semiotic functions (of which language is the most important) stresses their freedom from the spatiotemporal constraints inherent in sensorimotor intelligence. The intuitive child can adapt more effectively to her world than the baby can (or: she can effectively construct for herself a less limited world) because she can manipulate inner simulations, or representations, of actual and hypothetical situations. Thinking about doing something is usually swifter and often safer than doing it, which is doubtless why the semiotic function has evolved. And some things, such as the exploits related in fairy stories, cannot be done in the real world at all. The special importance of language (as opposed to imagery or mime) arises from the arbitrariness of the relation between signifier and signified. Not only does this mean that the words *cow* and *vache* (and countless others) can each be used to signify cows, but it also means that language can express abstract concepts such as justice, infinity and negation, which cannot be pictured or mimed in ways stable enough to function as a basis for extended thought or communication. For formal operational intelligence, which arises in adolescence, language is essential (though this is not to deny that some people find imagery useful in solving logico-mathematical problems).

The representations of the pre-operational child, however, are not so flexible or adaptive as those of the adolescent. We have seen, for example, that the six-year-old who can imagine making a necklace out of brown beads (and correctly predict that only a few white ones would be left)

P. — C

cannot integrate this representation with that symboliz-
ing her making a necklace out of wooden beads. Similarly,
even the child whose 'articulated' intuitions enable her to
match red and yellow sweets one-for-one cannot draw the
logical implication of the one-one representation – that
there are equal numbers of sweets in each row, even if
their spatial positions are now altered.

Piaget expresses this by saying that her intellectual
structures possess a lesser degree of equilibrium than those
of older, more logical children. But it is difficult to see
what this can mean, over and above the evident fact that
her thought and action are less well adapted to the real-
world environment than they will be later. Piaget's
language of 'degrees of equilibrium' implies that equilibrium can be measured in a given case, and usefully compared with its amount in other cases. One might speak in
this way of 'degree of equilibrium' in a homeostatic system
for regulating blood-temperature (taking into account the
range of blood- and external-temperatures compatible with
life), and compare individuals and species accordingly. But
we shall see in Chapter 6 that the broader notion of adaptation in general is very difficult to define (let alone to
measure) in biological terms. Psychological adaptation, or
Piagetian equilibrium, is no less difficult to define.

However, this does not necessarily mean that it is scientifically valueless or impossible to exemplify. Like its close
cousins 'adaptation' and 'feedback', Piaget's concept of
'equilibrium' may play a useful heuristic role in unifying
a large number of individual cases of more or less successful or well-regulated phenomena. If so, the detailed suc-
cesses and regulations concerned must be capable of
specification much as are individual cases of biological
adaptation or cybernetic feedback. Starting with a discussion of Piaget's account of operational intelligence, we
must now ask how this might be done, and whether
Piaget's formulation of equilibration can bear the theoretical weight he wishes to put on it.

4 Logic in Action

The paradoxes and seeming impossibilities of intuitive thinking start to disappear at about seven years, with the onset of what Piaget calls 'operational' intelligence. This newly developed understanding is made possible, he believes, by reversible operations integrated into systems that are logical structures. He claims that these enable the child to take account of mutually compensatory factors, and in general to realize implicitly the structural significance of the potential for reversing one's actions so as to restore some initial state. Despite the vagueness and incoherence of Piaget's abstract theory of operational thinking (which will be criticized presently), his research shows interesting changes in children's thought as they mature.

Initially, says Piaget, the developing operations are tied to practical, concrete situations: hence the term *concrete* operational knowledge (seven to eleven). The present and actual is well understood at this age, and the possible can be glimpsed as a practicable extension of it. But the possible is not fully appreciated until adolescence (eleven to fifteen) when *formal* operational thinking enables the abstract (propositional) representation of alternative hypotheses and their deductive implications. The possible is now seen not as a mere might-have-been (or might-have-done), but as the general structural limits within which the actual must necessarily be situated. As Piaget puts it, '*Possibility* [in adolescence] no longer appears merely as an extension of an empirical situation or of actions actually performed. Instead, it is *reality* that is now secondary to *possibility*.' [GLT 251]

To illustrate how the child's thought gradually becomes more logically structured and increasingly free of concrete situations, we may consider the example of seriation. Essentially comparable changes take place in other schemes, such as conservation, class inclusion, space, cause and so on.

In general, a seriation-task requires one to place in correct order the individual members of a set of items varying along a dimension such as length, weight, or age. For instance, a child may be asked to place a set of dolls or walking-sticks in order of length, or to thread differently sized beads so as to make a smoothly graduated necklace. And much scientific reasoning assumes a ranking of properties according to an ordinal scale, such that greater and lesser degrees of a property can be distinguished. Numerical scales (on which the degrees of a property can be measured and compared arithmetically) clearly involve seriation too. For, as Piaget points out, the scheme of seriation is an essential component of many complex types of thinking, including the understanding of number (to which class-inclusion also contributes).

After puberty, seriation problems can be solved abstractly, by transitive inferences within a formally conceptualized dimension (whether in everyday or scientific contexts). But prior to this, the domain must be concretely present if the child's seriation is to succeed. Even so, the youngest children cannot seriate in any but the very simplest situations, so that the middle-sized doll may not be given (put into one-to-one correspondence with) the middle-sized hat or walking-stick, largely because the 'middle' items are not correctly identified in the first place. What Piaget terms Stages I, II and III in the development of seriation behaviour [CCN Chs. 5 & 6] correspond respectively to the pre-conceptual, intuitive and concrete operational periods.

For example, the Stage I (pre-conceptual) child, of three or four years, is quite unable to build a 'staircase' of blocks with a set of seven blocks provided for her. The youngest children merely align the blocks in an arbitrary order.

An older Stage I child may construct two or more very short series (of only two or three blocks) which she is unable to integrate, or may build a single (short) series by simply omitting some of the blocks available. The Stage II (intuitive) child, of five or six years, is by contrast able to construct a perfect staircase using all of the seven blocks. But she does so by using what Piaget terms *trial and error*, choosing the next block virtually at random (except that she may pick one of the extremes as the starting-block). And she is unable to insert extra blocks into the staircase after she has finished building it.

Only at Stage III, with the development of concrete operations when the child is seven or eight years old, can she build a staircase by reliably starting with the longest (or shortest) of the seven blocks and then systematically adding the nearest in size. And only now can she correctly insert intermediate-sized blocks into a pre-existing staircase. (Piaget remarks that even such a child regresses to the trial and error stage if given a set of ten or more blocks to start with – as you probably would yourself, especially if the blocks were fairly similar in size. In Chapter 7 we shall question whether this behaviour should really be termed 'regressive'.)

Experiments on weight seriation, wherein children used scales to weigh blocks, showed a similar developmental progression. But the stages were shifted two or three years later. Stage-shifts were observed also in the development of conservation (substance before weight, before volume). Such shifts, which Piaget terms 'horizontal décalage', mean that when one describes a child as having attained the concrete operational stage, one cannot infer that all concrete operational tasks (irrespective of content) could be equally well performed by the child. This décalage thus presents a theoretical anomaly to anyone seeing concrete operational behaviour as due to a quasi-monolithic set of operational structures that the child either has or lacks.

The development of seriation behaviour is paralleled by developments in memory (and comparable changes occur for other schemes). So memory cannot be sharply distinguished from intelligence, since 'the development of memory with age is the history of gradual organizations closely dependent on the structuring activities of the intelligence.' [MI 380] For instance, if a child is shown a set of seriated sticks, her memory of them soon after tends to represent them as the sort of structure that she herself would have built had she been asked to. So a four-year-old will not remember a staircase as a staircase, whereas an eight-year-old will.

Even more striking, if the child is tested again eight months later (during which time she may have developed from the pre-operational to the concrete operational stage), her memory of the set of seriated sticks may now be more accurate than it was before. These results may seem surprising until one recalls Piaget's picture of the mind as an active, self-regulating system. One merely has to assume that the child uses her newly achieved operational intelligence not only to structure her bodily behaviour and perception (in building and recognizing seriated sets), but also to reconstruct her existing memories and/or to regulate her active reconstructions of the past. Psychologists since Bartlett have viewed memory as largely a matter of active reconstruction on the part of the subject, organized by general schemata in the mind that interact with stored representations of specific past events. Piaget's added claim is that the general operative co-ordinations of schemata, as opposed to their specific figurative content, develop with age – with predictable effects (sometimes leading to error rather than accuracy) on the organization of memory, both in retention and in conscious recall.

(This distinction between figurative and operative knowledge is variously expressed by Piaget, as corresponding respectively to the passive and active aspects of knowing; to the imitative (accommodatory) and creative (assimilative) aspects; and to the data or content known and the procedures or transformations effected on it. Mental imagery in general – whether involved in perception, memory or imagination – is predominantly figurative insofar as one considers its content only; but changing or using the image involves the operative aspect of the mind. So operative knowledge is a feature of all developmental stages, and must not be confused with 'operational knowledge'. In his later writings Piaget distinguishes between *schemes* and *schemas*, corresponding respectively to operative and figurative knowledge.)

For Piaget, mature seriation embodies a psychological structure that is characteristic of operational intelligence in general. He attributes the greater success of the Stage III child, as compared with the more limited seriation ability of the Stage II individual, to a combination of logic and self-awareness:

> By *concrete operations* we mean actions which are not only *internalized* but are also *integrated* with other actions to form general *reversible systems*. Secondly, as a result of their internalized and integrated nature, concrete operations are actions accompanied by an awareness on the part of the subject of the techniques and co-ordinations of his own behaviour. These characteristics distinguish operations from simple goal-directed behaviour, *and* they are precisely those characteristics not found [in Stages I and II, when] the subject acts *only* with a view toward achieving the goal; he does not ask himself why he succeeds. [GLT 6]

So the child's purposive behaviour, which appeared and became increasingly differentiated in the sensorimotor period, continues to develop in later stages. The self-knowledge of the operational period can be used in integrating and criticizing behaviour, and (as we shall see in Chapter 7) this conscious self-monitoring develops by a progressive internalization of bodily action dialectically shaped by the environment: as Piaget puts it, 'consciousness proceeds from the periphery to the centre.' The individual's generation and control of purposes suited to her needs becomes still more powerfully adaptive in the formal stage, since purely hypothetical means and ends can then be conceived in a logically systematic fashion.

The first part of Piaget's definition of concrete operations cited above implies that the behaviour of the Stage III child involves an implicit understanding of integrally connected logical relations such as reciprocity, transitivity and reversibility. Thus the child who can seriate successfully must be able to think in terms of two comparisons at once: this doll is smaller than that one, but larger than that one. She must understand that 'smaller' and 'larger' are transitive relations, such that a block near one end of a staircase must be smaller (or larger) than *any* block that is farther away from that same end. She must appreciate that the operation of seriation is reversible: she could have started with the largest block instead of the smallest, or she could so rebuild the staircase now, and the result would still be a staircase – though maybe pointing in the opposite direction. And she must realize that the two relations are reciprocal: if that block is smaller than this one, then this block is larger than that one.

Additionally, she must have mastered the conservation of length, so that a doll whose feet (and head) are nearer the ground is not thereby seen as shorter than its doll-twin whose feet (and head) are higher up, or so that two blocks lying on the table can be compared in length irrespective of the positions of their ends. But Piaget attributes length-conservation to underlying operations of a very general sort:

Non-conservation of length [when one of two equal sticks is moved forward on the table] is attributable to the absence of an independent reference system to provide a spatial framework for moving objects. Children who fail to establish paired relations between the two extremities of a moving object, will also be unable to link objects to reference elements. They cannot, therefore, take into account stationary 'sites' as distinct from moving objects. Without such a stationary medium which is essential to the intercomposition of distances and lengths, judgements of the latter can be expressed only in terms of the relative positions of their leading or trailing extremities. [CCG 98]

So 'additionally' was perhaps a misleading word with which to start this paragraph, since conservation itself involves some of the same logical operations that are essential to seriation. This is to say that in Piaget's view of intelligence the child's schemes develop in co-ordination, not merely in parallel. His extraordinarily ingenious and wide-ranging experiments tackle many different schemes, including those concepts that have traditionally been regarded as epistemologically crucial by philosophers. But his theoretical analysis posits shared underlying logical structures that not only generate but also co-ordinate them.

This co-ordination into an organized system ('structure') is supposed by Piaget to account for the essential novelty of operational thinking. For example, unlike P. Bryant (mentioned in Chapter 3) Piaget believes that reversible transitive inferences appear only at the close of the pre-operational stage, as newly developed concrete operations. The operational schemes of a single time, space and number-continuum are systems which integrate and thereby reconstruct the child's prior intuitive understanding of distinct temporal, spatial and numerical relations. The Stage III child understands (by reversible transitive inference) that the middle blocks in a staircase *must* be intermediate in length between those on either side, whereas the Stage II child knows (by inspection) merely that they *are* so related to their neighbours. Similarly, the operational child realizes that the water-level *must* be identical to the previous level if water is poured back into a jar, but the pre-operational child simply intuits that it *will* be.

According to Piaget then, the process of 'reflective abstraction', by which the transformational properties of the intuitive child's actions are internalized as logical thought, does not merely *repeat* these actions but *reconstructs* them systematically at the operational level. Despite his many statements that development is a continuous dialectical process, Piaget believes that there is an essential difference or logical discontinuity between successive stages. In his words, 'The various [operational] transformations involved – reversibility, combination of compensated relations, identity etc. – in fact depend on each other and, because they amalgamate into an organized whole, each is really new despite its affinity with the corresponding intuitive relation that was already formed at the previous level.' [PI 141]

By a further process of reflective abstraction (which it is easier for Piaget to name than to explain), concrete thinking later gives rise to formal intelligence. The adolescent (eleven to fifteen) can reason abstractly, since she can formally conceptualize possible transformations and their results (instead of having to imagine them figuratively or carry them out physically). That is, she can apply operations to operations, so that she can reason about her own reasoning independently of figurative (e.g. perceptual or semantic) content. Moreover, according to Piaget, she can do this in a systematic and logically exhaustive fashion, so that every possible transformation is allowed for.

Piaget sees this sort of hypothetico-deductive thinking as the intellectual core of the pinnacles of human knowledge: science and mathematics. And this formal operational competence not only dictates the logical structure of experiment and theorizing, but in so doing it also effects a further reconstruction of the child's existing schemes — such as cause, space, time, number and classification — which are central to her mature understanding of science and everyday matters.

For instance, the concrete operational child faced with a problem requiring causal analysis will attempt to experiment in an organized way, rather than rely (like the pre-operational child) on unsystematic trial and error. To this extent, her understanding of causal relations (or of the concept of cause) is more powerful than at earlier stages. But she is likely to repeat some combinations of transformations while omitting others, especially if some factors of potential causal relevance are not visible or readily distinguishable from others. Consequently, she often fails to identify the cause. The adolescent, by contrast, can hypothetically plan a series of experimental transformations such that complex causal relations can be deduced even when different substances are perceptually identical and experimental trials differing in theoretical significance have the same observable result.

An example involving causal reasoning is the Piagetian problem in which the child has to mix several colourless fluids so as to get the colour yellow. [GLT, Ch. 7] To cut a complicated chemical story short, if fluids from flasks 1 and 3 of the four flasks containing perceptually indistinguishable fluids are combined, and a few drops (similarly indistinguishable) from a smaller bottle are added, the mixture turns yellow; any other combination of the five fluids provided gives a colourless mixture. This problem involves not only positive but also negative causal dependencies, in the sense that the yellow colour can be cancelled by the bleaching effect of certain fluids. Piaget reports that, although they do not always manage to solve it, adolescents typically tackle this problem systematically, trying to investigate all possible combinations of the five fluids. When they do succeed, their hypothetico-deductive strategy enables them to understand the inter-related causal necessities involved. (This of course does not imply an understanding of the general chemical principles by which the theoretical chemist explains this phenomenon.) A younger child who, by great good luck, happened to combine the crucial fluids on her first trial would have 'found' the cause of yellowness, but would not have understood it fully as a cause.

Adolescent logic is not a mere accessory tool, to be wheeled out for use in tricky situations like the five-fluid problem. It is the active process by which the person constructs her entire world, such that she 'conceives of the given facts as that sector of possible transformations that has actually come about.' [GLT 251] Proceeding *from* what is possible *to* what is empirically real (instead of vice versa, as in previous stages) is 'the most distinctive property of formal thought'. [GLT 251] Piaget sees the familiar adolescent idealism (including his own, expressed in his early novel and prose-poem) as a 'belief in the omnipotence of reflection' that is a natural result of the need to exercise one's developing logical powers, in accordance with the principle of functional assimilation. It is as though the adolescent were intoxicated with logic, and adolescence is therefore 'the metaphysical age *par excellence*'. [6PS 64] (Piaget sees this as an adolescent egocentricity, which through interaction with the real socio-political world develops into a mature acceptance of the practical limitations on idealism; not surprisingly, he is charged with conservatism by critics of a more impatient temperament.)

However, logic is often more evident in intention than achievement (in Chomskyan terms, actual performance differs from underlying competence). This is to say that we often make logical mistakes, so that the five-fluid problem is not always successfully solved. Piaget is not committed to the obviously false claim that adolescents and their elders are paragons of logical rectitude. His point is rather that they appreciate the relevance of logical considerations to problems (whether expressed in concrete or abstract terms), that they can sometimes achieve a correct understanding of the solution (and of its justification) by logical reasoning, and that in general they understand that *there are* structured relations of logical necessity between propositions which define the range of possibilities within which the truth must lie. Finding the truth can therefore always be a rational hope, if one too rarely satisfied. But largely because his psychological theory is secondary to his epistemological interests, Piaget often writes (for instance in describing development on the five-fluid problem) as though the average person typically reasons in a way that would not disgrace a professor of formal logic.

What is more, his apparent assumption that systematic combinatorial search is the pinnacle of intelligence is itself questionable. To take just one example, chess masters (and even chess-playing computers) neither *do* nor *could* choose their moves by exhaustively considering all the possibilities. Rather, they use (fallible) rules of thumb, and rely on (sometimes misleading) analogies with past examples, including perceptible 'patterns' of pieces on the board. So despite his admission that thinking is maximally efficient only in areas of special interest and expertise, [HD] Piaget is commonly accused of overestimating the influence of deductive logic and neglecting that of less universally valid forms of reasoning in everyday thinking.

He is accused also of exaggerating the autonomy of logical development, and so underestimating the effect of social factors such as language[1] or logically structured teaching in secondary schools.[2] But nonliterate bushmen reason hypothetico-deductively when discussing hunting, which suggests that formal operations may be a feature of the adult mind even if they are not specifically encouraged and broadened in scope by Western academic education.[3] And some experimental attempts to induce operational thinking 'before its time' suggest that, while a child on the brink of the concrete operational stage can indeed be nudged across the stage-boundary by appropriate (practical and linguistic) teaching, children less advanced in their intellectual development cannot. These children may show a spurious, largely verbal 'development' which breaks down when the crunch comes, since it is not based on a genuine structural understanding. For example, children can apparently be taught weight-conservation prematurely, so that they give the right answers to 'Is it the same?' – questions about the weight of a lump of Plasticine alternately shaped as a snake or a ball. But if the experimenter cheats by surreptitiously removing some of the Plasticine while reshaping it, the younger children – who Piaget would say have been trained before they were ready – will accept the apparent non-conservation of weight (suggested by the perceptibly different levels of the scale-pans) with little surprise and no protest. The genuinely operational children, by contrast, refuse to accept the evidence of their senses and say things like 'You must have dropped some under the table.' However, non-Piagetians believe that other methods of teaching might succeed where these attempts failed, and some recent research on teaching concrete operations to young children suggests that this is so.[4]

This freedom from the senses is characteristic of operational thinking (which is why empiricist epistemologies are so embarrassed by the necessities of logic and mathematics). Piaget attempts to explain logic's independence of perception in terms of the high degree of equilibrium of operational systems. And he tries to explain the development of operational intelligence by the organism's natural tendency to move (by way of successive 'reflective abstractions') toward ever-increasing levels of equilibrium. Degrees of equilibrium, for Piaget, correspond to the availability of compensatory transformations, or structural reversibility: 'a system is in equilibrium when a perturbation which modifies the state of the system has its counterpart in a spontaneous action which compensates it.' [GLT 243] (Piaget thus identifies equilibrium with stability, as do many social scientists who use the term; but in physics a system may be in equilibrium, yet also be unstable, as is a ball resting on a flat surface.) For Piaget, equilibrium implies the ability to compensate for disturbances.

For example, to the extent that a (pre-operational) child is incapable of realizing the logical implications of a perceived change in water-level she is not in equilibrium, since the perturbation in perceptual evidence is not compensated for by a spontaneous mental action (operation) on her part. Physical action, however, can afford her a certain degree of equilibrium, in the sense that it can reverse the change in water-level so as to restore the perceptual input to its initial state. This purposive physical reversibility is itself developmentally based in the primary circular reactions of the Stage II sensorimotor baby, whose systematically repeated action-patterns evince a higher degree of equilibrium than the isolated reflexes of the newborn baby. The formal operational intelligence does not have to act out reversibility in the real world, or even imagine doing so figuratively, but can compensate by abstract realization of the logical relations between a proposition and its negation, double negation and so on. It is because the reversible and compensatory relations of logic are understood to apply to propositions in general, irrespective of content, that formal operational thinking is independent of perceptual evidence or empirical truth. Formal operational thinking, according to Piaget, has achieved a perfect equilibrium.

Although even sympathetic readers of Piaget sometimes dismiss his concept of equilibrium as 'surplus baggage', I suggested in the previous chapter that the idea of greater and lesser degrees of equilibrium may be heuristically useful in psychological and biological contexts. When we come to discuss Piaget's views on biology and cybernetics, we shall see that equilibrium in its various forms (such as homeostasis, homeorhesis and informational feedback – all of which will be explained later) is a function of the organism's power to adapt to environmental changes and inner perturbations so as to maintain its essential structure and natural life-history. An analogous concept at the metaphysical level is Spinoza's *conatus*, defined as the organism's attempt to persist in its own being. If Piaget's idea of psychological equilibrium (which is the weakest link in his theory) is to be more empirically useful than Spinoza's metaphysical analogue, it must sooner or later be complemented by detailed specifications of the 'perturbations' and 'compensations' actually involved. Piaget's theory of the abstract structures and transformations of the various developmental stages is an attempt to provide such a specification, and his notion of 'perfect equilibrium' is articulated in terms of his logical-algebraic theory of formal operational thinking. So his concept of equilibrium is well-specified only to the extent that this theory is acceptable. (Strictly, one should also mention his recent book on the mechanisms of equilibration [DT]; but we shall see that the most important criticism of his more well-known theory applies equally to this recent work.)

Faithful to his early passion for logic, Piaget expresses his theory of operational intelligence in a highly formalized manner, drawing heavily on the concepts and symbolisms of logic and algebra (though deforming them incoherently, as we shall see). He identifies his formalist aim as 'to study the applications of logical techniques to the psychological facts themselves, and especially to the thought structures found at different levels of intellectual development . . . The algebra of logic can help us to specify psychological structures, and to put into calculus form those operations and structures central to our actual thought processes.' [LP xvii] And the 'algebra of logic' offers us not only precision but humanity, for it enables a 'qualitative' (and by implication, relatively humane) analysis of the structures underlying intellectual operations, as contrasted with the 'quantitative' (positivistic, or behaviourist) treatment of their behavioural outcome: 'Most "tests" of intelligence measure the latter, but our real problem is to discover the actual operational mechanisms which govern such behaviour, and not simply to measure it.' [LP xvii]

So Piaget believes there is a mathematically expressible (and psychologically significant) qualitative analogy between the child who can describe the path from school to home *only* while she is at school (and vice versa) and the child who thinks there are more yellow sweets than red ones if the row of yellow sweets is stretched out. The progression from pre-operational through concrete to formal intelligence is characterized by him via distinct logico-mathematical structures of transformation (such as groups, groupings and lattices) having increasingly powerful mathematical properties (such as reversibility, commutativity and combinatorial richness).

For example, Piaget attempts to describe adolescent intelligence in terms of 'the system of sixteen binary operations' and the 'INRC group', which he says are based respectively on the logician's propositional calculus and certain transformations defined in elementary algebra.

Broadly, the first of these deals with combinatorial possibilities, and is appealed to by Piaget in explaining the adolescent's approach to hypothetico-deductive problems in general. He claims that, given two propositions each of which might be either true or false, the adolescent can systematically generate *all* the possible logical relations that might be inferred to hold between them on the basis of specific (experimental or informally arrived-at) observations. [GLT, Ch. 17]

The second (the INRC group) defines abstract operations or transformations having the algebraic properties of *I*dentity, *N*egation, *R*eciprocity, and *C*orrelativity (or in-

P. – D

version). [GLT 134, Ch. 17] These operations form a structure in the strong Piagetian sense, for they are logically inter-related so as to form a complete and closed reversible system : successive transformations can get one from any point within the structure to any other and back again. For Piaget, this means that they are in perfect equilibrium. He claims that the child's operational understanding of Plasticine (like the adult scientist's understanding of matter in general) involves an appreciation of the integrated structural possibilities defined by the INRC group. It is partly by way of Reciprocity, for instance, that the child comes to understand that increased width of a Plasticine snake compensates for decreased length; Correlativity enables her to realize the significance of the fact that a thin snake can be fattened and then thinned out again; and the relation of these operations to the Identity transformation (which leaves everything as it was before) accounts for her understanding of the conservation of the Plasticine's substance, weight and volume. Piaget defines logical (and psychological) equivalence relations between combinations of the four operations, such that $NR=C$, $CR=N$, $CN=R$ and $NRC=I$: these are supposedly analogous to the equivalence relations between the basic transformations allowed in algebra. [GLT 321]

It is easy to get lost in the formalist thickets of Piaget's discussions of groups, groupings, lattices, the INRC operations and the sixteen binary operations. Even professional logicians may be bemused, one such reviewer having complained, 'One must protest against so much ambiguity and obscurity in the use of logical symbolism.'[5] And the specifically psychological value of Piaget's theory is implicated in this complaint, which continues : 'It must be understood that these considerations are not just of exposition but of logical and, as we shall see, psychological substance . . . What fails to make logical sense can hardly make psychological sense in a study of intellectual development.' If, as logicians claim, Piaget's sixteen binary operations not only fail to get the propositional calculus right but are internally inconsistent in any case, they cannot reflect the combinatorial reasoning involved in hypo-thetico-deductive intelligence. (The defence that psychology must explain inconsistent as well as valid reasoning is not open to Piaget, who presents his theory as an epistemological justification of science and logic.) Understandably, then, while some Piagetians struggle to apply his 'algebra of logic' to their experimental work, others (and non-Piagetians in general) tend to skate over its formalistically expressed details.

Recent experimental research (much of it inspired by Piaget's pioneering studies) suggests that quite apart from his detailed formalisms, he may be criticized for concentrating too much on the psychological significance of abstract logical structure while tending to ignore the effect of concrete content and context. At the formal operational level, for instance, hypothetico-deductive thinking does not operate irrespective of specific content. Two problems of identical logical form may be easy or difficult, depending respectively on whether they do or do not tap familiar situations prompting commonsense reasoning of a context-dependent type.

For example, it is extremely difficult for people (including professors of logic) to guess which of four cards (showing the symbols A, D, 4 and 7 on their uppermost faces) would need to be turned over to determine the truth value of a sentence expressing an abstract and arbitrary rule such as, 'If there is a vowel on one side of a card, then there is an even number on the other side.' But most adults have no difficulty at all with problems of identical logical form if they are given envelopes (not cards) and rules like, 'If an envelope is marked PRINTED MATTER REDUCED RATE, then it must be left open.' Specifically, a mere 19.3-per-cent success rate on the abstract task rises to a staggering 98-per-cent in the realistic situation.[6]

As regards the development of intelligence also, content may make a difference. For example, horizontal décalage (in which conservation of volume lags behind conservation of weight, which trails conservation of substance) suggests that tasks that are logically equivalent at a very abstract level of description are not psychologically equivalent at a level which takes content into account. Analogously, it has recently been found that the development of children's performance on class-inclusion problems shows a somewhat different organization of thought-processes from that of their performance on length tasks.[7] These differences are not predicted by Piagetian theory, since these two types of task are regarded by Piaget as being subject to identical (pre-operational and, later, operational) abstract structures, and are represented isomorphically in the more rigorous axiomatization of Piaget's theory produced by his colleague J.-B. Grize.

Significantly, the experiments in which these latter differences were found were guided by a process model of thinking (a model similar to R. M. Young's theory, to be outlined in Chapter 7). A process model not only describes structural features of thinking and the general nature of the operations whereby one structured state can be transformed into another (both of which Piaget attempts to do), but also specifies the order in which particular processes or operations are carried out – which, in turn, implies explicitness about the necessary preconditions and immediate effects of the various operations. And this implies explicitness about the internal representations (symbolisms, data-structures) that are used. Given that (as Piaget has always insisted) thinking is a structured activity guided by feedback, in which symbolic representations are mentally manipulated and transformed, what the psychologist needs is an information-processing theory wherein the processing is as carefully specified as the information. Because of its relatively static, logical-algebraic formulation, Piaget's theory – and tidied-up versions of it, such as Grize's – cannot provide this. Indeed, the experimenter who compared children's understanding of length and class-inclusion had initially worked with a 'logical' model similar in type to Grize's axiomatization, but later decided that this type of model is inadequate *in general* because it fails to take process sufficiently into account. His final theory was influenced by computational ideas which, as we shall see later, are specifically designed to express dynamic processes of symbolic transformation.

However, even if one criticizes both the general nature and the details of Piaget's algebraic theory, one must appreciate the depth and originality of his project. He was aiming for a precise and qualitative formal specification of the development and functioning of the structured mechanisms and transformational processes by which intelligence is generated. And his concept of equilibration, unsatisfactory though it undoubtedly is, was intended to express the self-regulating feedback processes involved. As Chapter 7 will show, computational ideas (historically based not only in logic and mathematics but also in cybernetics, which Piaget saw as the general science of equilibration) can articulate the inner dynamics of psychological feedback where Piaget's talk of 'regulations' and 'equilibrium' cannot. But it was Piaget who raised these questions and kept them alive (admittedly in a vague and largely non-testable way) in a period when the conceptual tools for their more precise and detailed formulation were not yet available. Psychologists today who share Piaget's aim should acknowledge that it was he above all others who first identified it as the central task of cognitive psychology. (Freud's theoretical aim was similar in many ways, though unlike Piaget he did not attempt a rigorously formalized precision.)

We have seen that Piaget's account of operational thought (in contrast with his work on sensorimotor and pre-operational intelligence) tends to *over*estimate the rationality of adult thinking. This is due partly to his interest in intellectual competence as opposed to intellectual performance: what it is optimally possible for a person to do, not what she actually does in a specific situation.

But it is due also to his 'evolutionary' view of human knowledge, wherein intelligence inevitably progresses by a self-regulating process to a higher level, culminating in the 'perfect equilibrium' of logico-mathematical thought. That is, it is due largely to his epistemological belief that a developmental psychology (combined with an evolutionary biology) can both explain and justify knowledge in the form of science and mathematics. His epistemology and biology have influenced his psychological theory, as well as vice versa. He would think it nonsensical for someone (whether psychologist, epistemologist, or biologist) to say, 'Let's forget about children's knowledge: I'm only interested in understanding adult knowledge.' For Piaget, the ontogenesis of knowledge reveals not so much its (contingent) history as its (essential) nature. In the next two chapters we shall see that his views on the justification and the inevitability of operational knowledge are disputed respectively by many philosophers and most biologists.

5 Piaget and Philosophy

Piaget undertook his psychological research in the hope of solving epistemological problems. These concern the nature, possibility and justification of knowledge. He believes that his psychological theory (particularly when placed in its biological context) has specific epistemological consequences, which have to be appreciated if it is to be properly understood.

The epistemological questions that Piaget believes his experimental psychology (and his biology) to have solved include the following. Is knowledge best understood in terms of structure, content or process? If all three, then how are they in principle related? Do we actively construct our knowledge ourselves, or is it 'given' to us (by God, biology or experience)? If we construct it, then how can we be sure that it conforms to external reality? What are the relative contributions to human (and animal) knowledge of innate principles and environmental input? Is it only possible to learn about the external world if the learner already knows a great deal about it? Is it possible, and if so how, for us to have objective knowledge? What is the nature of logico-mathematical knowledge? Is it necessarily true, and if so where does its necessity come from? Can such necessity be learnt? How is it that this highly abstract knowledge applies to concrete things and actual events? Is language necessary for logical thought? Are there particular notions that are basic to human knowledge (if so, which are they: cause? object? space?), and are such notions innate in the newborn baby? What is meant by the concept of cause? Could a recognizably human mind exist in a wholly non-material universe? Could a broadly normal human mind exist in a body

totally paralysed from birth? Is it possible that there
might have been a world in which there evolved all the
living species we know about – with the exception of
any creatures capable (like us) of knowing the necessary
truths of logic?

Piaget's answers to most of these questions have already
been stated or implied, for one cannot formulate his psychology without suggesting answers to them. People with
no interest in philosophy as traditionally conceived become involved, willy-nilly, in epistemological enquiry if
they take Piaget's psychology seriously. Because of his
view of the relation between science and philosophy,
Piaget would say that the same applies to anyone who
takes any psychological theory seriously. But someone
might be unaware of this, especially if the theorist concerned was a positivistically inclined behaviourist who
proclaimed that psychology has at last freed itself from
philosophy and become a science.

Piaget thinks of his developmental psychology in the
light of traditional philosophical positions. He sets out the
historical opposition between empiricism and rationalism
(recently stressed in less clearly dialectical terms by
Chomsky[1]). Empiricism, he says, describes the growth of
knowledge in terms of genesis without structure, whereas
rationalism offers us structuralism without genesis.

Empiricists such as Locke and Hume rightly saw that
rationalist accounts of 'innate ideas' put an implausibly
heavy weight upon mental preformation, or what Leibniz
termed 'pre-established harmony' between the subject's
knowledge and the known reality. Why should innate
ideas conform conveniently to reality?; and even if they
did, how could we *know* that they do except by experience? In addition, they realized that deductive speculation alone cannot suffice to solve epistemological problems. So Piaget praises them for raising 'fundamental and
fruitful enquiries' and for appealing to a largely genetic
psychological science 'whose scope [they] only glimpsed

and which did not as yet exist.' [IIP 53, 54] With the comparatively recent rise of associationist psychology and behaviourism, empiricism was at last given proper experimental expression.

Nevertheless, says Piaget, empiricism's doctrine of the featureless mind or *tabula rasa*, which passively accepts experiental input and whose knowledge is therefore a copy of the world, is false. So its epistemology is unacceptable also : empiricists fail to see that 'knowledge constructed by the subject is not due to experience alone, and that in general it always involves a structuring of which empiricist philosophy has not seen the extent nor grasped the full import.' [IIP 54] For example, empiricism cannot give a convincing explanation of the necessity of logic. Some early empiricists (notably J. S. Mill) represented logical principles as the result of inductive learning. But $2+2=4$ appears not to be true if one is playing with mercury droplets; and even if it always happened to be true, wherein would its necessity lie? If knowledge is a mere copy of reality, passively accepted from outside, how is it possible for it to transcend our spatiotemporal environment? Piaget concedes that the later empiricists (logical positivists) did try to do epistemological justice to logic, differentiating it from inductively learnt empirical knowledge so as to explain its necessary character. But they wrongly 'tried to reduce it to a language', [IIP 55] and so not only made claims that conflict with Piaget's psychological research on the relation of language and thought, but also left entirely mysterious how it is that mere linguistic conventions or empty formulae can apply so usefully to the physical-world.

Rationalism, by contrast, rightly stresses the contribution of the knowing subject and recognizes the need for logical principles prior to experience. Piaget sees Leibniz as especially significant, because of his insightful defence of the anti-empiricist position that there is indeed nothing in the mind prior to experience – except the mind itself,

which must be so structured as to be able to organize experience meaningfully. (Even the 'empiricist' Hume accepts this, in that he posits innate psychological tendencies
governing the association of ideas; but he does not em-
phasize these organizing principles as Leibniz does, and
denies that there is any informational content innate in
the mind.)

But in addition to the problem of pre-established harmony already noted, rationalism has other difficulties. It
implies that the principles of logic – as opposed to more
primitive principles of assimilation – are innate. Why
then cannot babies do algebra? Rationalists (such as
Descartes, Leibniz and Plato) offer various answers, all
claiming that in some sense the baby needs experience to
activate, realize or be reminded of the innate ideas of
algebra or logic. But like Locke before him, Piaget is un-
persuaded by such answers: 'observation and experiment
show as clearly as can be that logical structures *are* constructed, and that it takes a good dozen years before they
are fully elaborated.' [S 62] In an attempt to explain the
peculiar nature of logical knowledge, Piaget says that processes of reflective abstraction and equilibration (the first
o^f which is not needed for sensorimotor learning) give rise
to logico-mathematical structures having 'that necessity
which a priorist theories have always thought it necessary to posit at the outset. Necessity, instead of being the
prior *condition* for learning, is its *outcome*.' [S 62] Whether
such obscure processes as these can indeed explain the
nature of logical necessity is doubtful, however: are they
made any clearer by Piaget than *anamnesis* by Plato?

Classical (and some modern) rationalists and empiricists
share two philosophical biases that set them at odds with
Piaget. First, many of them ignore mental processes and
structures which, like those posited by Piaget, are not
consciously introspectible. Phenomenologists and existentialists show their common Cartesian origin in this way,
although the self-styled 'Cartesian' Chomsky does not.

And even ordinary language philosophers often dismiss inferred cognitive processes and structures as 'myths'.[2] Second, classical rationalists and empiricists underplayed the role of bodily action in the growth of knowledge. For Descartes, indeed, to whom mind was wholly distinct from matter and could in principle exist without it, Piaget's suggestion that human knowledge – even including logic – could be explained by reference to our biological embodiment and infantile gropings would have been absurd.

Piaget's epistemological synthesis is a genetic structuralism 'very close to the spirit of Kantianism'. [IIP 57] For, like Kant, Piaget stresses the constructive activity of the mind in the formation and interpretation of experience, and believes that we must experience in terms of certain structural principles if we are to experience at all. But whereas Kant ignored questions about the development of the forms and categories of space, time, identity and cause – all of which are essential to adult subjective experience and objective knowledge – Piaget does not. He argues that the baby does not have concepts of cause or identity equivalent in organizational power to the adult's, but has to develop them from primitive beginnings by successive cycles of interaction with the environment. And although Piaget regards the development of logicomathematical knowledge as an inevitable end-result of equilibration (in the individual or in society as a whole), he does not view Newtonian physics and Euclidian geometry as necessary features of objective knowledge, as did Kant who lived before the theory of relativity and geometries of non-Euclidean space. However, Piaget agrees with Kant that logical and mathematical systems, or sets of necessary truths, are not arbitrary 'analytic' conventions but constructions having genuine 'synthetic' intuitive content insofar as they reflect experienced properties of the real world.

Piaget's dialectical synthesis of empiricism and rationalism, which respectively provide insights about the content and structure of experience, is therefore similar in its general philosophical nature to Kant's arguments about the possibility of knowledge.

Kant's distinction between the experienced world of *phenomena* and the transcendental world of *noumena* expressed a strongly idealist streak in his thinking (later developed by the German ¹dealists). He regarded the objects in the experienced world as phenomena caused by underlying things-in-themselves (noumena), which exist independently of our senses but of which we can know nothing except their empirical appearances. These appearances are inevitably structured by features of the human mind (which in other rational beings might be different), such as the forms and categories of space, time, cause, identity and so on. Kant could distinguish between the 'unreal' horse one rides in a dream and the 'real' horse one rides in a meadow, because only the latter is an object of intersubjective agreement between different minds. But the reality of the horse is empirical rather than transcendental, and what we call 'knowledge' can be only of empirical (experienced) phenomena, not of their transcendental causes. It is hardly surprising that Kant's philosophy gave way to a full-blooded idealism, as later thinkers rejected the noumenal world as metaphysically superfluous.

Piaget is aware that as a constructivist he must be careful to avoid idealism – or, to put it another way, that he must answer the sceptic's challenge that perhaps all our so-called 'knowledge' is mind-dependent illusion. He tries to buttress his commonsense realism by appealing to the biological basis of knowledge:

> To attribute logic and mathematics to the general co-ordinations of the subject's actions is not an idealistic overestimation of the part played by the subject; it is a recognition of the fact that, while the fecundity of the subject's thought processes depends on the internal

resources of the organism, the efficacy of those processes depends on the fact that the organism is not independent of the environment but can only live, act, or think in interaction with it. [BK 345]

In a sense, this realist attempt to explain the objectivity of knowledge in terms of its biological provenance is the Piagetian equivalent of Dr Johnson's kicking a stone in 'refutation' of Bishop Berkeley (for whom 'to be is to be perceived'). But Dr Johnson underrated Berkeley, who would have predicted the pain in the toe and the thud of the stone on the ground. And the anti-Piagetian idealist or sceptic would question Piaget's biological notions of 'organism' and 'environment' just as much as his psychological notions of 'logic' and 'schemas'. Idealism cannot be refuted so easily as this, and Piaget remains open to the charge that he cannot justify his realism.

But three things can be said in Piaget's defence. First, many philosophers refuse to embrace idealism even if they cannot produce knockdown arguments against it (G. E. Moore specifically said this was the intellectually respectable thing to do[8]). Second, many psychologists with constructivist leanings do not appear to notice the epistemological problem, which Piaget tries to avoid by his appeal to biological factors.[4] And third, Piaget defines psychology as the science of 'implicatory' rather than 'causal' relations. [FP 186-9] As we shall see later, this accords well with a basically materialist philosophy – and corresponding forms of biology and psychology – that is neither reductionist nor idealist. It is not reductionist, since it distinguishes cognitive processes ('implications') from their material embodiment ('causes'), and – like Piaget – sees psychology as grounded in but irreducible to physiology. Nor is this approach to knowledge idealist, since it takes for granted both the underlying physiological mechanisms in which knowledge is grounded, and the survival function of knowledge for the cognitive system in interaction with its enviroment. According to the constructivist perspective, this taking for granted is entirely justified at the empirical level. But whether it is justified at the transcendental level also is an obscure and highly controversial matter, which even Kant failed to settle. In short, all the theoretical psychologies based on notions such as *construction* (and *representation*) are flirting with idealism, and Piaget's is no exception.

In general, Piaget's account of science is non-reductionist, in that he does not believe (as positivists do) in a theoretical unity of science such that all the special sciences could in principle be replaced by a basic science, physics. But his anti-reductionism is coloured by his Kantianism, so that he says:

> Psychology thus occupies a key position [because] if the sciences of nature explain the human species, humans in turn explain the sciences of nature, and it is up to psychology to show us how . . . It follows that the system of sciences cannot be arranged in a linear order . . . [but their form] is that of a circle, or more precisely, that of a spiral as it becomes ever larger. In fact, objects are known only through the subject, while the subject can know himself or herself only by acting on objects materially and mentally. [AP 651]

Even in his philosophical novel of 1918, Piaget had sketched the circle of sciences in which 'the laws of one science are founded on another', [G 45] so that we pass in turn from psychology to the underlying biology, thence to chemistry, physics, mechanics and logic – and so to psychology again.

Sociology and the moral sciences (what Piaget now calls 'philosophy' proper, or the study of wisdom) lay outside the main circle, being a level above biology but side-by-side with psychology; but later he said that 'every psychological explanation comes sooner or later to lean either on biology or on logic (or on sociology, but this in turn leads to the same alternatives).' [PI 3] As these differing positions suggest, Piaget's attitude to sociology is somewhat equivocal. And he is often criticized for underestimating the importance of interpersonal and group influences on the child, and for ignoring the wider social context. He does not wholly neglect these matters: he admits that different cultures and educational practices will affect the rate of development of intelligence, and in his early psychological work he stressed factors such as the influence of the child's peer-group. He has even acknowledged that 'society is the supreme unit, and the individual can only achieve his inventions and intellectual constructions insofar as he is the seat of collective interactions that are naturally dependent, in level and value, on society as a whole.' [BK 368] But society and individual, he continues, are like the chicken and the egg: each depends on the other and 'there are not two kinds of logic, one for the group and the other for the individual . . . Cognitive regulations or operations are the same in a single brain or in a system of cooperations.' Despite these remarks (and similar statements of the importance of motivational factors as opposed to 'purely cognitive' ones), Piaget concentrates first and foremost on cognitive regulations within individuals. Those philosophers who take social roles and cultural milieu to be largely definitive of (not just causally related to) what in classical liberal terms is 'the individual', and who insist that *objectivity* itself is an irreducibly social concept, are therefore critical of what they see as Piaget's overly individualistic approach.[5]

In answering epistemological questions, Piaget refers to his psychological research, which he calls 'experimental epistemology'. But an experimental epistemology (whether his or anyone else's) can be acceptable only if his views on the relation between philosophy and psychology (or, more generally, science) are correct. As he is well aware, these run counter to 'the traditional philosophical view of epistemology'. [GE 1]

Piaget deplores the tendency of philosophers in general to undervalue the philosophical significance of science, and warns against entrusting epistemological questions not to professional scientists but to 'philosophers, who think themselves capable of judging such cases without any technical training.' [BK 343] Continental phenomenologists and existentialists, no less than Anglo-American logical positivists and linguistic philosophers, regard scientific findings as in principle irrelevant to philosophical problems. This deliberate separation of philosophical from scientific enquiry is based in explicit philosophical doctrines such as : the phenomenologist's focus on essences introspectively intuited by the method of conscious bracketing; the positivist's distinction between cognitively meaningful science, tautologous logic and metaphysics; and the linguistic philosopher's differentiation of questions about language or concepts from questions about facts.

Accordingly, the Continental approach to philosophical psychology assumes that there is a purely reflective way of reaching knowledge about the mind, in which empirical enquiries like Piaget's are deliberately 'bracketed' out. And the Anglo-Americans likewise regard psychological facts about the history of a concept or belief as in principle irrelevant to its philosophical justification or epistemological worth. As a result, such philosophers often feel that there is no need for them to read Piaget – and if they do, they accuse him of systematically committing the genetic fallacy.

In general, the genetic fallacy is to think that one can justify some belief (or impugn its validity) simply by detailing its history. For instance, those people who say (as Freud did not) that its psychological origin in the Oedipus Complex shows theism to be false are committing the genetic fallacy. And so, according to many philosophers, is Piaget when he says that 'Genetic epistemology attempts to explain knowledge, and in particular scientific knowledge, on the basis of its history, its sociogenesis, and especially the psychological origins of the notions and operations upon which it is based.' [GE 1]

D. W. Hamlyn, for example, despite his strong sympathies with Piaget's epistemological position and with his critiques of classical empiricism and rationalism, insists that 'philosophical questions about the nature of a certain form of understanding and about its conditions and criteria are utterly divorced and distinct from psychological questions about the conditions in which such understanding develops in individuals.'[6] It is not that he thinks Piaget to have nothing of philosophical interest to say: but Piaget's empirical psychology (or biology) cannot settle any of his epistemological questions, and a 'theory that rests directly upon both empirical and philosophical considerations must have a degree of incoherence.'[7]

Such criticisms are in order insofar as they point out specific failures on Piaget's part to distinguish as clearly as possible (which is not necessarily to say, sharply) between conceptual and empirical questions. They are even 'scientifically' helpful in doing this, for they are relevant to questions about the degree to which Piaget's claims are in principle falsifiable. For example, Hamlyn's discussion of Piaget's claims about the (necessary or contingent?) ordering of developmental stages is useful in this regard. Even a Martian baby could not be in sensorimotor Stage 5 before 4, because the concept of 'searching for a means' includes that of 'means'. We do not have to study Martians to find this out. But this does not mean that Piaget's discussion of Stages 4 and 5 is trivial. Conceptual truths may be hidden, and their empirical illustration can be instructive. (Conversely, of course, good concepts can illuminate the empirical material.) It is logically possible that Stages 4 and 5 might have appeared together instead of (as Piaget's observations suggest) successively. Moreover, only empirical study of normal and handicapped babies can show *which* means the baby can employ and search for (sensorimotor ones), or which circumstances and actions seem to aid the transition from Stage 4 to Stage 5. Finally, only observation can provide specific examples of the ways in which abstract principles (such as reversibility or causality) are in fact foreshadowed in human babies – these might be interestingly, though they could not be entirely, different in Martians.

But criticisms claiming the irrelevance of empirical considerations to philosophy apparently forget, what Piaget himself points out, that the most important systems in the history of philosophy have all arisen from reflection on scientific discoveries. The philosophies of Descartes, Locke and Kant – to take a nicely dialectical trio – are cases in point, and Piaget cites many more.

'Purist' philosophers of course concede that empirical facts and scientific concepts have been and remain heuristically useful in the formulation of philosophical theories, spurring the re-examination of conceptual presuppositions and suggesting possible alternatives. They would not deny, for example, that the conceptual formulation of the philosophical mind-body problem from the seventeenth through to the twentieth century clearly reflects the history of technology : clocks, steam engines and computers. But such purists would not accept Piaget's claim that scientific investigation can show a philosopher's conceptual scheme to be so ill-fitting with the facts that to continue to adhere to it is to be intellectually perverse and irresponsible. Even the anti-positivists among them would insist that the logical positivist's view (that logic is based merely in linguistic conventions) need not be given up because of anything that Piaget may find his prelinguistic children doing.

Piaget admits a distinction between facts and norms (which latter include not only moral values but normative logical principles), and agrees with the purist that 'proceeding from a fact to a norm . . . is certainly inadmissible.' [IIP 103] Philosophers who have tried to base theoretical logic too directly upon 'natural logic' (that is, the way most people in fact reason) are accused by Piaget, as by the purist, of falling prey to 'psychologism', the attempt to settle questions of validity by considerations of psychological fact. [IIP 66, 103] And he concurs with the purist that:

> Insofar as any attempt to solve a logical or mathematical problem by using results borrowed from psychology is called 'psychologism', we likewise condemn psychologism without hesitation, for it shows a confusion not only of the methods but also of the questions themselves. In effect, if the logical problem, in the case of a mathematical demonstration, consists in discovering under what conditions it can be accepted as valid, the psychological problem consists only in determining by what mental mechanism it actually develops in the mathematician's mind. [ME 132]

However, epistemology is no more identifiable with logical axiomatics (which deals with formal validity) than with purely empirical psychology (which describes actual thought mechanisms). For epistemology is traditionally concerned with the possibility of the realization (the existence) of valid knowledge, not with the formal demonstration of its logical validity as such. 'Knowledge' is itself a hybrid concept, involving both psychological and rational considerations (which is why it is often defined as 'justified true belief'). It follows that epistemology must be a dialectic co-ordination of insights drawn from logic and psychology. In expressing this view, Piaget offers two main reasons why scientific psychology is – *pace* the purist – relevant to epistemology. First,

> even in mathematics . . . the [normative] concept of self-evidence changes throughout history, and sometimes as a result of sudden intellectual crises. How can we

therefore refuse to acknowledge that the way in which a self-evident judgment is formed can elucidate its soundness or weakness according to whether, for example, it is related to the very general co-ordinations of actions and operations, or whether it depends, like certain out-of-date self-evident judgements of geometry, on limiting factors of perception or imagery rather than on these constant operational co-ordinations? [IIP 190]

Second, and a generalization of the first point, the growth of knowledge 'always simultaneously gives rise to questions of fact and norms', so that epistemology must combine the normative approaches of 'logic, which no one would question in its specialized form', and of the empirical 'history of ideas and the psychology of their development'. [IIP 76] Only such an interdisciplinary methodology can do justice to the continuing dialectic between epistemological fact and epistemological norms in the ontogeny and phylogeny of human knowledge. (However, Piaget's many suggestive comparisons between children's thinking and the history of physics and mathematics are inadequate in various ways. For instance, he ignores the influence of the social context in raising questions within these disciplines, and also misunderstands the nature and historical importance of mathematical *proof*.[8] The latter failing is especially relevant here, since it is developments in mathematicians' concepts of proof that establish mathematical 'norms' at a given time.[9])

For these two reasons, then, epistemologists must take account of the actual thought mechanisms that make the realization of knowledge possible. At any given time, realization and validity can be distinguished; but the development of the relevant notion of validity was itself a real epistemological process, which needs to be understood in psychological terms. Even though there is no possibility of a straightforward *contradiction* (or, conversely, relation of *proof*) between scientific psychology and justificatory axiomatics, there comes a point at which empirical evidence may render a philosophical doctrine or epistemology (such as logical positivism, or phenomenology) so implausible that it cannot be responsibly adhered to. This can happen because all epistemology brings up factual problems as well as formal ones, and 'The first principle of genetic epistemology, then, is this – to take psychology seriously. Taking psychology seriously means that, when a question of psychological fact arises, psychological research should be consulted instead of trying to invent a solution through private speculation.'[GE 9] So Piaget attacks philosophical schools that show a 'reactionary' and 'aggressive' spirit with respect to young sciences, saying that they should pay more attention to the rational 'values of objectivity and painstaking verification'. [IIP 211]

In view of his 'disenchantment' with philosophy [IIP xvi] it is ironical that some critics of Piaget say in effect not *He is a scientist, not a philosopher* but *He is a philosopher, not a scientist*. Like Freud, Piaget has fierce critics who seem to believe that all his distinctive hypotheses fall into one of two classes: falsifiable, and indeed false; and unfalsifiable, so scientifically empty. Such people conflate individual criticisms and complain that his descriptions of what children can and cannot do are banal or false ('where there are developmental changes, they are the opposite of those suggested by Piaget'); that his theory of stage-ordering is tautologous ('logical truths dressed up in psychological guise'); and that his explanatory concept of equilibrium is so vague as to be theoretically useless ('surplus baggage').

But one should remember that even Popper, whose philosophy of science makes falsifiability essential to scientific theories, does not necessarily write off unfalsifiable theories as scientifically valueless. (Though he does criticize 'scientists' who turn a falsifiable theory into an unfalsifiable one by endlessly postulating *ad hoc* hypoth-

eses, or continually redefining their terms, in the face
of apparent falsifications.) An unfalsifiable theory, which
is metaphysical rather than scientific, may act as a powerful heuristic in directing pre-scientific conceptual speculation that later can be applied in a more scientific manner.
So the Greeks propounded many metaphysical theories,
such as atomism and heliocentrism, which helped keep
alive ways of asking questions that turned out later to be
of enormous scientific significance. Piaget himself makes
the similar point that 'We have today [thanks to cyber-
netics] a scientific concept, and no longer a metaphysical
one, corresponding to finality [purpose] (which positivism
would never have foreseen, since by limiting scientific problems, it would never have made such hypotheses).' [IIP
42] Still less should one scorn falsified hypotheses. For the
fallibilist Popper, science can progress only by way of conjectures *and refutations*.[10] And even if one's philosophy of
science is non-fallibilist, in asserting the epistemological
possibility of knowing what *is* the case, one must allow
that it is scientifically valuable to know what is *not* the
case. So if one were to believe (in my view wrongly) that
Piaget's work is compounded only of false experimental
hypotheses and unfalsifiable theoretical claims, it still
would not follow that it must therefore be mere mistake
and metaphysics, and of no scientific importance. (It must
be admitted, however, that Piaget's methodology does not
encourage the systematic search for counterexamples.)

Although Piaget does not believe – as phenomenologists,
for example, do – that there is a specifically philosophical
way of arriving at knowledge about the mind (or anything else), he does assign an important substantive role
to philosophy. He sees it as concerned not only with
'knowledge' (science and/or genetic epistemology) but also
with 'wisdom' (values). Anything which counts as knowledge must, for him, be scientific. Although in his first
two books he aimed to reconcile science with values –
specifically, with socialism and Christianity – he later

concentrated on knowledge alone. He left the articulation of wisdom, and its rational co-ordination with knowledge proper, as vital problems to be solved by philosophy. Philosophy in this sense is not objective, as science is, because values are not intersubjectively verifiable – so that 'there can be several wisdoms, while there exists only one truth.' [IIP 210]

The nature and existence of this assumed distinction between science and values is more philosophically problematic than Piaget implies.[11] One might be tempted to say that nothing specifically Piagetian hangs on this issue, while allowing that Piaget like any other psychologist is open to questions about the moral-political content and context of his theories. For example, he has been criticized on 'moral-political' as well as on 'factual, scientific' and on 'purely epistemological' grounds for emphasizing the individual person at the expense of the social milieu in his account of the growth of objectivity.[12] And he has been accused of conservatively and pessimistically implying (what J. S. Bruner, for instance, denies) that certain things simply cannot be taught to children at a particular stage of development, so that there is no point in trying. (Rebutting the charge of pessimism, Piaget replies that 'genuine optimism would consist of believing in the child's capacities for invention. Remember also that each time one prematurely teaches a child something he could have discovered for himself, that child is kept from inventing it and consequently from understanding it completely. This obviously does not mean that the teacher should not devise experimental situations to facilitate the pupil's invention.') [H 715]

But Piaget is more open than most psychologists to the charge that he should not take the fact-value distinction for granted. For we saw above that Piaget thinks that scientific facts are *not* irrelevant to or clearly distinguishable from epistemological justifications. Even though logical axiomatics (which deals with 'validity or values' [ME 140]) can be considered entirely apart from 'natural logic', the notions of logical truth and objective knowledge are firmly grounded in epistemologically relevant facts about the structure and development of the co-ordinations of operations within the epistemic subject. That is why, he believes, his psycho-biological theories can explain the nature and objectivity (not just the origin) of knowledge. But to call an aspect of the mind 'knowledge' (rather than 'belief' or 'faith', which Piaget uses for moral-ideological commitments) is to value it as rational, to regard it as epistemologically justified. So in claiming that psychology is essential to epistemology, Piaget is in effect claiming that *rationality as evaluative* at least cannot be sharply separated from scientific facts.

Although he distinguishes wisdom and truth, Piaget says they are not in principle opposed. There can be 'rational beliefs' [IIP 218] (and even formalizations of ethics, or a 'logic of values' [IIP 67]). But philosophy cannot be defined as rational belief because some philosophies are strongly irrationalist. Piaget confesses to a 'complete aversion with respect to existentialism, which blurs all values and degrades man by reducing freedom to arbitrary choice and thought to self-affirmation.' [IIP 218] But he confesses also that his own belief in freedom is a matter of wisdom (even though it takes psychological knowledge into account) rather than knowledge.

Questions about the relation between philosophy and science 'touch the roots of our ideologies', largely because at the sociological and individual levels 'philosophical thought has become either a substitute or a necessary support for religion', and so attracts the same strong personal commitments. [IIP xv] Existentialism, phenomenology, Marxism, Christian theocentrism and logical positivism are examples of socially influential philosophical systems used in these ways. And some of these systems claim the status of 'knowledge', or even of 'science'.

Philosophical systems such as these are of immense

social importance because they present (differing) claims
about the nature of man. Piaget insists that any intellectually honest philosophical anthropology must take account
of psychological science. For psychology illuminates
notions like objectivity, rationality, constructivism, nativism, freedom, purpose and the conscious-unconscious
distinction – all of which are controversial terms within
philosophy as a whole. But philosophical anthropology
must also take biology seriously. Many people accuse
contemporary 'sociobiologists' of demeaning human
nature, and criticize their theories on scientific grounds
wherever possible so as to avoid what they see as their de-
grading philosophical implications.[18] For Piaget, however,
biology does not demean human nature but exalts it.
Occasionally he expresses this view with regard to problems typically discussed by sociobiologists, saying for
instance (what sociobiologists usually deny) that 'the more
one examines the mechanisms of life, the more one discovers that love and altruism – that is, the negation of
war – are inherent in the nature of living beings.' [G 41]
More characteristically, he relates biology to epistemological problems. Biological principles, he believes, not
only guarantee 'the harmony of mathematics with the
real world', [BK 339] but also show the rise of logico-
mathematical knowledge to be a necessary crowning of
the whole evolutionary process.

6   Piaget and Biology

Piaget says that his psychology 'is impossible to understand if one does not begin by analysing in detail the biological presuppositions from which it stems.' [H 703]

He does not mean merely that he is a 'biological' psychologist in the most obvious sense. True, he never loses sight of the fact that human beings are biologically evolved creatures with material bodies, endowed from before birth with specific motor and sensory mechanisms through which they will interact with their environment. If these mechanisms were very different, then 'our cognitive universe would be very different . . . our fundamental concepts would be turned upside down, not just because of the way things appeared to us but because of our means of action.' [BK 271] His biologist's sensitivity to this fact is largely responsible for his outstanding contribution to our psychological understanding of sensorimotor intelligence, as well as for his insistence that epistemology be based in sensorimotor knowledge. The sensorimotor capacities of the newborn baby are themselves developed from the movements and responses of the foetus, the biological study of which is 'an embryology of reflexes' that will eventually be integrated into developmental psychology. [PC vii] And Piaget sees comparative psychology as a valuable endeavour, citing the development of object permanence in kittens – and even the visual illusions of minnows – in his brief 'summing-up' of his work in child psychology. [PC 15, 38]

But even more significant here is Piaget's conviction that the biological problem of adaptation relates to psychological and epistemological problems about the nature and possibility of knowledge. Consequently, theoretical biology is an essential part of genetic epistemology.

And epistemology is no less essential to biology: Piaget criticizes most biologists for not asking 'whether the adequacy of knowledge to objects could be brought back into their explicatory schema' of evolutionary adaptation. [BK 67] The view that epistemology is none of the biologist's business is due, he says, to the tendency of neo-Darwinism and positivism alike to think of knowledge as being based on simple copies of reality, passively absorbed from (and naturally reflecting) the environment. If knowledge is instead conceived of as the active assimilation of input by the autonomous structures of the organism, then questions arise about the nature and origin of these structures and about their ability to generate maximally adaptive constructions of external reality. These questions now facing the biologist, whose concern is adaptation, are the central questions of genetic epistemology.

Piaget sees the problem of integrative stage-by-stage development in the child's intelligence as 'an extension of the problem embryologists raise when they wonder whether ontogenetic organization results from pre-formation or from epigenesis, and what causal processes are involved.' [PC 153] The distinction between pre-formation and epigenesis in embryology rests on a dialectical opposition between two poles of biological theory — Lamarckism and Darwinism — and a synthesis in terms of 'epigenetic assimilation'. This strikingly Piagetian vocabulary is in fact drawn from the biologist C. H. Waddington, whose book *The Strategy of the Genes* (1957) was seen by Piaget as a detailed vindication of his own longstanding general approach to biology.[1] For Piaget, the dialectical opposition between Lamarckian and Darwinian biology is analogous to that between empiricism and innatist rationalism in psychology and epistemology.

'The two central ideas in Lamarckism,' says Piaget, 'are the part played by the exercise of the organs during development and the fixation in heredity of the modifica-

tions thus brought about (heredity of "acquired" characteristics).' [BK 105] That is, features adaptively (and even
intelligently) developed in response to the environment are
biologically transmitted to the offspring. Clearly, Lamarckism allows in principle for the evolution of knowledge –
and Piaget agrees with the spirit of both 'central ideas'.
But he accuses Lamarckism of tending to see 'nothing but
the effect of the environment (the organism, for him,
makes no reaction except to acquire "habits" which are
more or less forced upon it).' [BK 106] An extreme version
of Lamarckism therefore cannot give due weight to the
interactions between organism and environment, or to the
specific contribution from the nature of the organism
itself. It is non-Kantian with respect not only to human
intelligence but also to embryology, for it cannot recognize the largely autonomous morphological development
of the embryo – including the remarkable ability of embryonic tissue to compensate for experimental perturbations (such as bisection of the embryo or transplantation
of cells from one part of the embryo to another) so as to
preserve the structural integration of the embryo as a
whole.

Darwin himself believed in the inheritance of acquired
characteristics (though he did not regard it as the most
important evolutionary process) – and reasonably so, since
the genetic theory of his time posited a plausible mechanism. Copies of cells from adult organs were believed to
migrate in maturity to the gonads, there somehow fusing
to form sex-cells. If this were so, the adult characteristics
(which might have been heavily influenced by environmental factors and even by intelligent adaptation to them)
could be passed to the offspring.

But with the rediscovery of Mendelian genetics at the
turn of the century, a mechanism of inheritance was
posited which denies the possibility of any such direct
environmental influence on the genetic material, or
genome. According to neo-Darwinism (Darwin-plus-Men-

del) the hereditary material is already present in the organism before birth; although random environmental influences (such as radiation) can effect mutations in the genes, there is no way in which the environment can directly effect biologically adaptive changes in them. Moreover, orthodox molecular biology sees the development of the fertilized ovum as a more or less automatic process, wherein the messages precoded in the DNA of the genome are 'translated' into the proteins of the embryonic cells. Certainly, the gene-protein translation may go wrong (with good or, more usually, bad effects for the whole organism); and the environment then plays a crucial role in selecting some organisms (or gene-populations) rather than others. But this environmental selection is entirely *post hoc*, and provides no pressure on the organism to develop or the species to evolve to a higher level of adaptation. Hence Piaget's term 'preformationism', and his objection that Darwinist 'mutationism' is too random to explain the evolution of knowledge.

Even in his early writings Piaget sought a biological *tertium quid* (expressed in terms of assimilation and accommodation) that would allow the mutual interactions of organism and environment to have evolutionary – and epistemological – significance. [G 40-1] And he claimed to find experimental evidence for his theoretical approach in his observations of variation in animals and plants. For example, he studied the pond snails in various' Swiss lakes (transferring some snails from one lake to another), finding that the morphology of the shell was adaptively – and inheritably – altered by environmental factors such as depth and water conditions. [BK 300-4] He claimed that this change in the shape of the shell happened by way of the sensorimotor adaptations made by the snail in moving its muscles so as to resist the agitation of the water, which adaptations somehow (he did not clearly say how) caused inheritable changes in the genome. (Orthodox Darwinists would say that only those snails were able to

survive which fortuitously happened to be already genetically destined to make those movements and grow those
shells which in fact had survival-value in the turbulent
water.)

Piaget sees his pond snails as lowly analogues of human
babies. For he cites these experiments in the context of saying that he had 'always thought it impossible to explain
innate sensorimotor behaviours without this hypothesis
o. the inheritance of acquired characteristics, and this is
particularly so in the case of the (absolute) reflexes which
are the most important sensorimotor reactions of the
first year.' [6PS 117-18] Elsewhere, he argues that the
inner 'logic' of instinct is 'closely connected with the
forms and schemata of sensorimotor intelligence.' [BK 264]
The newborn baby, for Piaget, is as she is because her
sensorimotor capacities have evolved in a 'Lamarckian'
fashion in human and pre-human species.

Piaget's psychology thus involves the biological claim
that there are inheritable interactions between the developing organism and its environment (or between the gene-
pool and the ecological niche of the evolving population).
And for Piaget, morphogenesis must therefore be the crux
of evolutionary theory. Morphogenesis is the development
of the embryo from a single undifferentiated cell to an
organized whole of mutually co-ordinated structures (the
bodily organs). But prior to his reading of Waddington,
Piaget's theoretical remarks about evolution were highly
schematic in character, identifying assimilation and accommodation in broad terms as 'the functional invariants
of intelligence and biological organization, . . . the invariants common to all structuring of which life is
capable.' [OIC 3] His genetic structuralism in biology
attempted a synthesis of the Darwinian stress on the
organism's autonomy and the Lamarckian emphasis on
the organism's adaptive response to the environment. But
it did not clearly describe a mechanism whereby adaptively
acquired characteristics could be inherited. This is what

Piaget takes Waddington to have done.

For Waddington too, morphogenesis is central to evolution. It is because he sees evolution as due largely to systematically adaptive (embryonic and adult) responses to environmental influences that Piaget praises him for 'making phylogenesis depend in part on ontogenesis, and not only the inverse.' [BK 81] Waddington's theory of (epi-)genetic assimilation assigns evolutionary significance not only to the genotype and the environment – as does neo-Darwinism – but to the phenotype also. The phenotype is the organism's observable form, its structural morphology and behaviour patterns, whereas the genotype is its stored genetic information. Selection operates directly on the phenotype. Waddington points out (what no Darwinist would deny but which many seemingly ignore) that any one genotype is sufficiently flexible in its developmental potential to allow for a number of morphologically and behaviourally different phenotypes. Which one will in fact develop depends on the reciprocal relations between the developing organism and the environment.

The notion of reciprocal interactions is crucial here (and Waddington criticizes orthodox neo-Darwinism for holding to a linear model of causality whereby such processes of systematic mutual regulation cannot be represented). If the organism happens – either by extraneous chance or as a result of autonomous 'choices' or regulations – to find itself in environment X, then its phenotypic development will very likely be adaptively affected accordingly. For within limits, the genotype has the potential of generating distinct structurally self-maintaining phenotypes that actively compensate for the particular features of that environment. These differentiated phenotypic structures are not merely responses to the environment, but alter the environment in developmentally significant ways. To take an example from embryology, a very early embryonic cell has the potential of becoming a muscle cell or a neurone; depending on its spatial position in the embryo as a whole and/or its biochemical environment, it will develop into one or the other; once it has developed (with its neighbours) into muscular or nervous tissue, it influences further development by acting as part of the morphogenetic environment for other cells, so that they form into muscles or neural organs (or their appropriate neighbour-organs, such as tendons or vertebrae) respectively.

Thus the phenotype should not be seen (as neo-Darwinists tend to see it) as a mere surface manifestation of the underlying genotype, which latter suffices to express the essential nature of the organism. Rather, the phenotype should be recognized as the result of a multi-levelled and self-regulating developmental process, that integrates environmental perturbations (and random genetic mutations) into an orderly sequence of 'sensibly' structured developmental changes. Organism and environment together form one unitary system (as is emphasized at the species-level by ecological biology).

To characterize the nature and limits of developmental potential, Waddington sketches a metaphorical 'epigenetic landscape'. The ball in Figure 1 represents the developing organism (which may be thought of at the level of the cell, the organ, the individual or the species). The layout of hills and valleys is genetically determined, and varies between individuals.

The valleys represent 'chreods', or 'necessary paths', along each of which the ball may potentially travel but on only one of which it can be at any given time. The chreods impart their characteristic properties to the ball as it passes, and the valley-depth represents the degree of difficulty the ball would have in leaving one path in favour of another. This picture thus schematically represents the fact, for instance, that a cell cannot develop both muscle and nervous proteins at the same time, that it can initially be easily triggered (pushed) into developing either of these, and that as differentiation proceeds it becomes more and

Figure 1. **The epigenetic landscape**

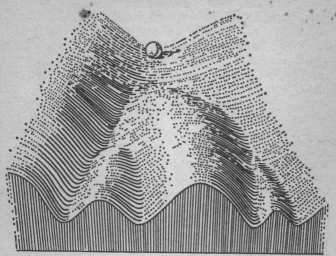

(Source: C. H. Waddington, *The Evolution of an Evolutionist*)

more difficult for it to switch (either spontaneously or under environmental influences) from one to the other. The location of valleys (which ones are next to which) can be used to represent the relative ease or probability of developmental process X giving way to developmental process Y or Z. And the location of cols connecting neighbouring valleys can be used to represent the critical periods during development at which sudden changes can occur.

A real ball pushed up the side of a hill will naturally fall back into the valley again and proceed on its way, thus compensating for the perturbation and preserving its initial trajectory. Note that it does not preserve its initial *state*, or position, but its initial process, or trajectory. This is why Waddington calls the self-regulation of development 'homeorhesis', in contrast with 'homeo-

stasis' which acts to preserve a static or enduring con-
figuration rather than a progressively developing process.
Like homeostasis, homeorhesis is flexible only within
limits. Thus the difficulty of leaving a deep valley represents both the adaptive self-conserving autonomy of the
organism in face of many environmental (including experimental) perturbations, and its maladaptive inflexibility
in face of some threats to its integrity.

Waddington expresses the evolutionary significance of
his view by saying that the epigenetic landscape can be
altered by natural selection. Strictly, one should not think
(as Lamarck did) in terms of an individual organism trans-
mitting its phenotype directly to its offspring, but in terms
of populations having an 'average' epigenetic landscape.
Figure 2 shows an example of the modification of the
epigenetic landscape by selection. Every landscape contains potentialities for trajectories (including cross-col
journeys that involve switches from one path to a very
different one) that are not normally followed, but which
may be taken in response to novel environmental influences. Biologically significant examples include morphological changes, choice of new habitats and special forms
of behaviour. Those individuals whose landscapes contain
suitable potential paths (well-placed cols, for example) will
be able to adapt, and those who do so will survive to
leave offspring. After many generations, the population
will have a higher proportion of members with 'good' cols
(and a spontaneous tendency to pass over them) than it
had originally – which is to say that the average epigenetic
landscape of the population will have been adaptively
altered in response to environmental influence.

There are innumerable points in Piaget's later writings
which correspond very closely to Waddington's views –
not surprisingly so, since Piaget draws many of his theoretical claims, detailed terminology and illustrative examples directly from Waddington. What is relevant for
present purposes is the extent to which there are signifi-

Figure 2. **Modification of the epigenetic landscape by selection**

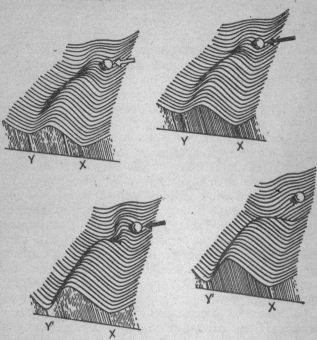

The upper left drawing shows the situation in the unselected foundation stock; a developmental modification Y will occur only if an environmental stress (white arrow) forces the developing system to cross a threshold or col. The upper right figure shows the Baldwin-Lloyd Morgan hypotheses – that a new gene mutation (black arrow) appears which substitutes for the environmental stress, everything else remaining unaltered. The two lower figures show stages in the selection of genotypes in which the threshold is lowered (requiring only a 'small' gene mutation or, eventually, a single specifiable mutation) and the course of the developmental modification is made more definite and directed to the optimal end-result, Y'.

(Source: C. H. Waddington, *The Evolution of an Evolutionist*)

cant parallels between the independent approaches of the two writers, and to what extent Piaget differs from Waddington.

Waddington shares with Piaget a fundamental theoretical bias toward interactive processes in biological explanation. He has even admitted recently that 'my particular slant on evolution – a most unfashionable emphasis on the importance of the developing phenotype – is a fairly direct derivative from Whiteheadian-type metaphysics', suggesting as an illuminating caricature of Whitehead's metaphysics the view that 'there are no things, only processes'.[2] In the next chapter we shall see the importance for Piaget of the discovery of regulatory genes, and of his remarks (with which Waddington would entirely agree) that 'genes are not a series of motionless little balls but essentially processes at work throughout the whole of ontogenetic development', [BK 114] and that 'at every stage of development of the living structure . . . the essential question is that of the regulation mechanism.' [BK 12] It is because of his independent theoretical commitment to self-regulating systems, that Piaget welcomes Waddington's picture of the evolutionary system as 'four main subsystems [the self-regulating actions of genes, epigenetic system, environment, and natural selection] inextricably linked to one another by an overall system of cybernetic circuits.' [BK 12]

Piaget's assessment of his snail experiments as showing some sort of quasi-Lamarckian evolution is accepted by Waddington, who even commends them as 'the most thorough and interesting study of genetic assimilation under natural conditions.'[3] But he rejects Piaget's theoretical discussion of them on two counts. Piaget underestimates the role of natural selection and overestimates that of individual adaptation, because (*qua* biologist no less than *qua* psychologist) he tends to think in terms of individuals rather than populations. And for an essentially similar reason, Piaget is misled into postulating a too direct or Lamarckian influence on the genotype (which he tries to explain in terms of a mechanism vaguely described as a 'progressive reorganization, or gradual change in the proportion of the genome'). [BK 304] In general, Piaget overestimates the degree to which Waddington is a Lamarckian, and so overestimates the extent to which Waddington's work can support his own. Waddington describes himself as a 'post-neo-Darwinist', who tackles morphogenetic questions often ignored in modern biology without denying the basic tenets of Darwinism. So although he is unorthodox, and although his evolutionary views are (respectfully) criticized by 'mainstream' Darwinists,[4] Waddington is not so strongly opposed to Darwinism as Piaget is – or as Piaget sometimes takes him to be. [BK 175] From the point of view of genetic epistemology, however, the most important difference between the two men is that only Piaget believes in the evolutionary necessity of logic.

Piaget postulates an inevitable evolutionary progression (analogous to and in part comprised by the growth of human knowledge), criticizing Darwinism for not doing likewise. And just as human knowledge is said by him to develop inevitably toward greater equilibrium through processes of assimilation and accommodation, so evolutionary progress (or 'vection') is said to be the inevitable result of analogous processes of 'opening' and 'integration' respectively.

Opening is an assimilatory 'increase in the possibilities acquired by the organism in the course of evolution', which Piaget says leads to knowledge as 'a necessary final achievement, in that it multiplies the field of these possibilities.' [BK 123] The adolescent, for example, can rationally take into account hypothetical possibilities that cannot be clearly imagined by the concrete operational child; and the pre-operational infant can conceive of possibilities (such as an unseen object's being hidden under a cushion) beyond the ken of babies in the early sensorimotor stage. Analogously, evolutionary development of sense organs and motor functions effectively enlarges the actual and virtual environment of animal species. Integration, by contrast, is an accommodatory tendency 'making the development processes more and more autonomous in relation to the environment.' [BK 356] Examples include the evolution of physiological homeostasis (whereby the organism maintains a constant 'internal environment' such as blood temperature) and of biochemically based systems of embryological 'organizers' regulating the autonomous and complex development of the fertilized ovum – what Piaget, after Waddington, terms 'homeorhesis'. At the human level, integration results in cognitive structures defining an internal (mental) environment having a high degree of independence from the external world – namely, logico-mathematical knowledge. In life, of course, these two dialectically opposed tendencies are active together: a species' greater self-regulating integration provides for an increased openness to the potential implicit in its environment.

It is important to realize that the phrase 'in that' quoted in the first sentence of the preceding paragraph is ambiguous. Interpreted as 'because', it expresses a non-sequitur: for even if one were to accept that there is some form of lawful evolutionary advance toward greater equilibrium, and that degrees of equilibrium are both usefully measurable and inter-specifically comparable, it would not follow that any particular degree of equilibrium must necessarily be reached (except perhaps in the mathematical sense, in which parallel lines 'must' meet at infinity). Interpreted as 'it being true that', this phrase is in order: logico-mathematical knowledge does enormously multiply the range of (actual and virtual) actions that are possible for the organism. But this is to point out the (biologically adaptive) usefulness of such knowledge, given that it has arisen – it is not to prove from biological laws that it must necessarily evolve.

Most modern biologists would not accept Piaget's claims about the inevitability of the evolution of logico-mathematical knowledge. Some would even deny that any objective sense can be given to notions of evolutionary progress. (Piaget himself criticizes writers such as Huxley, who believed in inevitable evolutionary progress, for not giving a value-free definition of the term. [BK 122-3]) Others would admit that there has been progress, intuitively evident as an increase in 'adaptive complexity', without believing that this notion can be precisely defined so as to be theoretically useful.[5] A few have tried to define some general theoretical parameter (comparable to the physicist's entropy) that will always increase during evolution; for example, the 1960s saw proposals that homeostasis is always increased and that the efficiency of using limited resources continually improves.[6] Both these recent suggestions have something in common with Piaget's more explicitly cognitive view of an evolutionary increase in adaptive equilibrium. And Waddington similarly suggests as a criterion the ability to keep alive and leave offspring by exploiting available *and new* resources, answering those who would query the whole notion of evolutionary 'progress' by saying that 'we will take seriously the worm's claim to be our equals when the worms come and present it, but not before.'[7] But despite his impatience with those who would put us on a par with the worms, Waddington does not postulate the necessary evolution of human knowledge to the stage of formal logic.

This example of worms reminds us that there are many phylogenetically primitive species still extant. Neo-Darwinists (and Waddington), who can acknowledge progress if it occurs without regarding it as inevitable, are not theoretically embarrassed by this fact — but a necessitarian progressivist like Piaget should be. He cannot simply say that worms see some part of the truth and human beings another, so that the whole truth cannot be seen without both worms and humans existing; nor can he even say that worms see some of the same truth that we do, as might someone who 'defined truth as being that which there is in common between all the different views that all creatures, including man, have held about the world.' [BK 362] For Piaget claims that the evolutionary rise of knowledge (analogously to the child's progress from sensorimotor to operational thinking) involves not just the linear addition of new facts or forms but the dialectical *re*construction of the previously existing forms of knowledge (much as the adult's 'sensorimotor' intelligence is not identical with the baby's). This view – which he terms 'convergent reconstructions with overtaking' – implies that the worm's knowledge is retained in a superior, radically reconstructed, fashion in the cognitive structures of its evolutionary descendants. What need, then, for the inferior wormish forms to persist? If, as Piaget says, 'the very nature of life is constantly to overtake itself', [BK 362] why have not the worms been overtaken and left behind aeons ago?

Part of Piaget's admiration for Waddington derives from their common aim of bringing knowledge back into biology: 'A sort of revolution in our biological and our epistemological views has been brought about by Waddington's declaration . . . that no physical science can be complete so long as the term "Mind" (or mental life) is excluded from its vocabulary . . . Being a biologist whose work is inspired by cybernetics, he understands that no theory of organization and adaptation dares leave cognitive adaptations out of account.' [BK 67]

There are two senses in which one might seek to bring knowledge into biology, both of which are favoured by Piaget (and Waddington). One is to aim for a biological epistemology, and the other is to aim for a cognitive biology.

A biological epistemology is a theory of knowledge that, at the least, takes careful account of biological facts (such as the sensorimotor capacities of the baby), and at the most finds epistemological *justification* in the biological nature of the knowing subject. The justification of knowledge (and whether the genetic fallacy is a fallacy in epistemology) was discussed in Chapter 5, in the context of Piaget's developmental psychology. The points raised then apply equally in the context of his biology. For instance, Piaget identifies the fundamental operations of class inclusion (achieved by the 'operational' child) with hierarchical biological structures at many different levels: mature organisms, the genetic system, the developing embryo and so on. [BK 158] His point is not the idealist notion that, since we construct our knowledge ourselves, we naturally 'find' its properties in our theories about the biological world. Rather, it is the realist view that we are able to construct our theories in this way because as biological creatures we embody logically equivalent principles of organization, and we justifiably so construct our theories because they have been found throughout evolution to be fitted (interactively adapted) to the biological and ecological phenomena from which they spring. Moreover, the rise of objective logico-mathematical knowledge is seen by Piaget as a biological inevitability. Those philosophers who distinguish sharply between the genetic (scientific) explanation of knowledge and its epistemological justification regard Piaget's 'biologism' as equally suspect with his 'psychologism'. They would allow only that his biological discussions of lower organisms, as of the sensorimotor stage, might throw light on the nature and development of beliefs – which only a strictly epistemological account could justify as knowledge. Nor would they be prepared to ascribe knowledge to organisms that are unable to justify their beliefs by giving reasons – as must be done within a cognitive biology.

A cognitive biology would be one in which biological phenomena of all sorts were seen on the analogy with phenomena that clearly constitute knowledge. Morphogenesis in the embryo, for example, would be theoretically described in terms suitable also to the description of human cognition. Certainly, the distinction between the higher cognitive processes of the human mind and the 'cognitive' processes of embryological development would have to be noted. For instance, Piaget's claim that human knowledge (especially logico-mathematical knowledge) shows a greater dissociation of 'form' and 'content' than does the organization of a living thing [BK 152] would have to be retained in some such insight as that the embryo (unlike the mind) cannot 'refer to virtual as well as to actual events, hence to imaginable possibilities, . . . since it must actually realize any cognitive process it is engaged in.'[8]

Significantly, the latter quotation comes from a respected experimental biologist who is a pupil of Waddington, and who sees his own recent work as an extension of Waddington's suggestion that *language* may become 'a paradigm for the theory of General Biology'.[9] B. C. Goodwin's self-professedly 'cognitive' biology is consonant with Piaget's view that there are 'different levels of what may be considered to be cognitive functions on every rung of the animal kingdom, if no more.' [BK 62] For even slime moulds and bacteria are thought of as cognitive systems by Goodwin.

Goodwin's self-styled 'structuralist' discussion of cellular physiology and embryological development theorizes in the terms not only of molecular biology and mathematical models (including catastrophe theory, which deals with sudden stage-discontinuities) but also of 'cognitive systems' adapting and evolving on the basis of 'knowledge' about themselves and their environment.[10] The processes of embryogenesis and evolution are said to manifest creative intelligence (though most organisms are not themselves intelligent), and there is a cognitive continuum throughout the phylogenetic scale, from the lowliest living creature to human minds. Goodwin argues that the cell, embryo and adult organism should all be seen on the analogy of recent models of artificial intelligence (whose relation to cybernetic theories in biology will be discussed in the next chapter). That is, they should be thought of as hierarchical systems of co-operating cognitive units, communicating and interpreting coded messages that control the context-sensitive behaviour and structural transformations brought about on various levels by specific physiological processes.

To take the best-known example, DNA is not merely a biochemical substance (a string of four types of nucleotide) but a biologically significant semantic sequence, whose procedural meaning (commands specifying that *this* protein should be assembled, using *these* out of the twenty amino-acids, in *this* order, stopping at *this* point) is interrupted and affected by the overall epigenetic system of the developing cell. Comparable meaning is attributed by Goodwin to biochemical 'pacemakers' and 'organizers', which control the morphogenetic processes in embryos and regenerating creatures such as hydra.

Goodwin insists that he does not wish to use the notion of knowledge here in a loose, analogical sense, but tries to define knowledge in a rigorous and experimentally applicable way that will provide for fruitful comparisons between higher cognitive activities and biological processes. He defines knowledge as 'a useful description of some aspect of the world, giving the possessor the competence to behave in a manner which contributes to its survival and reproduction.'[11] The words 'description' and 'competence' are crucial here. Descriptions are structured expressions generated from codes, where a code is not a set of natural laws (such as the laws of physics or biochemistry) but a set of rules that may be and often are essentially arbitrary, but which can be interpreted in an appropriate context by a cognitive system as relating to specific processes or states of affairs. For example, there is nothing in physics or chemistry which says that a particular sequence of three out of the four nucleotide bases *must* correspond to (act as the coded message commanding the assembly of) a particular amino-acid. Yet in fact the evolutionary process has come to use these essentially arbitrary triple-nucleotide sequences in highly meaningful ways – 'meaningful' in that they allow precisely for the survival and reproduction of living creatures. Similarly, there is nothing inherently 'leggy' about a biochemical organizer which in fact elicits the formation of a limb-bud in the embryo. The word 'competence' is deliberately reminiscent of Chomsky's postulation of the adult's tacit knowledge of grammatical rules and the baby's innate language-specific learning system, and highlights the structured and creatively generative potential of what Goodwin terms 'knowledge'.

What is important here is the markedly Piagetian tone (and the largely Waddingtonian provenance) of this recent biological research. If even the metabolism of lactose by bacteria, morphogenesis in hydra, and the aggregation of slime moulds are processes of control best described in cognitive terms, and if extant species can fruitfully be seen (as Goodwin sees them) as 'the results of the working of an intelligent [evolutionary] system',[12] then Piaget's aim of unifying biology and knowledge by bringing knowledge into biology – not just by illuminating the biological basis of knowledge – is not so far-fetched as it may seem.

However, aim is one thing and achievement another: as well as clarifying some of the recent cybernetically-related ideas on which Goodwin and other biologists currently draw, the next chapter will show how Piaget's more classical cybernetic conception of equilibration fails to capture cognitive processes. It is because of this failure that Piaget cannot elaborate his suggestive remarks about 'comparative epistemology' [BK 62] so as to provide an adequately detailed theory of knowledge, whether at biological or physiological levels. A comparative epistemology of *time*, for instance, would need to be able to integrate Goodwin's work on cell growth and biological clocks with Piaget's research on children's ideas of temporal order, duration, and speed. To do this would require not merely more biological and psychological data, but a better appreciation than Piagetian theory offers of the complexity of 'equilibration' in cognitive processes. Piaget adopts the terminology of classical cybernetics, but I shall next suggest that recently developed concepts (currently being used in 'information-processing' or 'computational' approaches to psychology) may be more helpful in detailing the dynamic nature of equilibration.

7   Piaget and Cybernetics

Cybernetics is the science of self-regulating systems (whether living or not) that function by way of informational feedback. Although it originated in a technological context, it is not essentially 'about' machines, and its central idea of informational feedback is relevant to issues in biology, philosophy and psychology.

In view of Piaget's conception of biological and cognitive systems as internally regulated wholes, interacting dialectically with their environment, it is no wonder that he often refers approvingly to cybernetics. 'Life is essentially autoregulation,' he says, and 'cybernetic models are, so far, the only ones throwing any light on the nature of autoregulatory mechanisms.' [BK 26, 28] Or again, 'Cybernetic models . . . are of very special interest to us because they give a direct expression to the structures which are involved in all cognitive mechanisms.' [BK 61]

'Cybernetics' was founded in the 1940s by the mathematician N. Wiener, but its central idea had entered biology in 1866 with the work of C. Bernard and had been given further physiological specification by W. B. Cannon in 1932. Bernard's 'internal environment' and Cannon's 'homeostasis' were biological concepts marking the self-regulating equilibratory processes of temperature control, blood-sugar level and so on, which Wiener formalized in terms of 'informational feedback'. Wiener thought this notion to be as useful in psychology as in biology, since he believed that it made notions like *goal* and *purpose* clearly intelligible and systematically useable. Purposive behaviour, he said, was behaviour governed by negative feedback, using 'signals from the goal [that] restrict outputs which would otherwise go beyond the goal', and as a paradigm case he suggested a machine designed so as to impinge on a moving luminous 'goal' (the target).[1]

In such an example, the continuous calculations made as the moving machine approaches the target are carried out by a computer, whose function can then be described in cybernetic terms. The early cyberneticians W. R. Ashby and W. Grey Walter produced mechanistic theories of brain function and working mechanical models of lifelike ('goal-seeking') behaviour based on cybernetic principles. This type of cybernetics was more directly applicable to analogue than to digital machines, for the significant representational processes within an analogue model vary continuously (and measurably) rather than in discrete steps. But in 1943, W. McCulloch and W. Pitts exploited the analogy between the binary logical units of which digital computers were being constructed and the all-or-none firing of cerebral neurones. They described hypothetical neural networks having abstract properties akin to those of the logician's propositional calculus, and their ideas encouraged physiologists and psychologists to ask whether the epistemological functions of the human brain, or mind, could be modelled in a computer. The 1950s saw the first computer simulations of cognitive processes, while cybernetics in the form of General Systems Theory was applied by L. von Bertalanffy and T. Parsons to the 'open systems' of biology and sociology.[2]

Piaget's interests – whether in biology, psychology, sociology or logic – were naturally sympathetic to these developments, which promised a more rigorous formalization of his idea of self-conserving operational wholes. He remarked on the 'ingenuity' of Grey Walter's mechanical tortoises, praised McCulloch and Pitts for their attempt to explain logico-mathematical knowledge in terms of neural mechanisms, agreed with von Bertalanffy that equilibrium can be likened to a stable state in an open system, and welcomed the cybernetic account of homeostasis and biological organization in general. [e.g. G 754, BK 367, 6PS 101, BK 221-3] He repeatedly describes his epigenetic account of evolution and morphology in cybernetic terms (which Waddington does also), as one for which the evolutionary system (from genes to species) is 'an overall system of cybernetic circuits' on different levels. [BK 121] Genes themselves are not 'motionless little balls', but 'processes' involving 'regulation'; he cites the recent discovery of regulatory genes (which turn the action of other genes on or off, according to circumstance) as proving that cybernetic feedback functions even within the genome. [BK 114]

Passing from biological to psychological systems, Piaget was not misled (as some biologists were[3]) by Wiener's essentially *non*-psychological, *non*-subjective, definition of 'goal' or 'purpose'. Wiener's so-called 'goal' was the target itself – but the mere fact that our goals are often never achieved (and are sometimes inachievable) shows that 'goal' or 'purpose' is a psychological concept, and involves the subject's having an *idea* of what it is that she proposes to do. It is this subjective idea that governs, or regulates, purposive behaviour, with the help of any relevant feedback of signals from the material world (as also from within the mind itself) that may be available. This is why Piaget insists that behaviour in sensorimotor Stage 2 is not purposive, and that true intentions are seen only in Stage 4. In using the cybernetic notion of environmental feedback to explain intelligent behaviour, Piaget did so in the context of his psychological theories about the subject's inner constructions of reality. What information will be actively sought out, and what effect it will have within the organism, depend on the way in which feedback is regulated by the mind's action-schemata and operational structures.

Feedback, then, is a process that can occur in various domains, involving assimilation and accommodation of appropriately varied kinds. As Piaget puts it when discussing the functioning of genes, 'It is the property of a regulation, *in every sphere*, to feed information to the system in action about the results of its actions, and to correct them in terms of the results obtained.' [BK 114, italics added] Piaget says of the (non-formalized) biological work of Bernard and Cannon that it had prepared the way for 'a rethinking of causality along the lines since followed by cybernetics.' [BK 129] The cyberneticians' philosophy of life and mind involves a 'cyclic causality', [BK 131] where the focus of scientific concern and theorizing is not a linear series of successive events so much as a system of transformations within an overall organization, one that is regulated by feedback of information. (In Chapter 6 we saw that Waddington similarly criticizes neo-Darwinists for their linear concept of cause.) For Piaget, cybernetics provides the dialectical core of a general theory of equilibration.

A general theory of equilibration must be able to deal with the feedback of information in specifically psychological systems as well as biological ones. A recent development of cybernetics (drawing heavily on logic and mathematics) that concentrates on psychological questions is artificial intelligence ('AI'), which is no more 'about' machines than is cybernetics in general.[4] AI is a way of studying intelligence that uses computer programs to aid discovery of the thought-processes and epistemological structures employed by intelligent information-processing systems (whether living or not). This new type of cybernetics differs from classical cybernetics in important ways (so much so that, despite the historical connections, the word 'cybernetics' is often understood to exclude AI by people – like Goodwin – dissatisfied with the classical variety). Specifically, AI programs are information-processing systems whose self-regulation *cannot* helpfully be described in terms of the sorts of algebraic concepts and equations favoured by Piaget, and by the many biologists (whom he commends) using classical cybernetic models in theorizing about genetics and ethology.

The reason for this is that the cybernetician's 'feedback' (which in classical cybernetics is defined and measured in terms of *quantitative* information) appears in AI as a wide variety of *qualitatively* distinct informational tests and monitoring routines, inter-related in flexible rather than fixed ways. These are used for assessing and reducing the discrepancies between actual (or hypothetical) and desired states, and they often involve complex inferential processes and changes in the existing knowledge of the system. An AI system realizing the impossibility of reaching a toy itself, for example, could integrate its general and specific knowledge to infer that its best strategy might be to ask some other system (the mother?) to get the toy; programs capable of this type of problem-solving may also take into account the fact that some 'third-party' systems need to be bribed or threatened to help them fulfil their own goals, while others can be relied on to help without special sanctions. As this example shows, the information that is fed back is often semantic rather than numerical information. Consequently, its use during the self-regulatory feedback process cannot be expressed by a purely quantitative mathematics of 'positive' and 'negative' feedback but must be marked by computational, or programming, concepts. It is because these differ so from the concepts of classical cybernetics, which deal with measurable information passing along fixed pathways or 'circuits', that AI is often regarded as a development *from* cybernetics (together with logic) rather than a development *of* it, and as having escaped the constraints of quantitative science.

Computational concepts are not concerned with counting (as the word 'computational' may suggest), but with *any* rule-governed symbol-manipulation. This is why many cognitive psychologists believe them to be capable of describing thoughts and thinking. They are specifically designed to mark the procedures by which information of various kinds can affect and be integrated into cognitive structures of differing types. For instance. they deal with the search for, the sudden noticing of, the acceptance and appropriate passing on of, the comparison between and inference from, and the transformation of items of information – both from within and from outside the information-processing system as a whole. This is to say that they are designed to express the inner processes of accommodation and assimilation. By contrast, the algebraic concepts used by classical cybernetics – and by Piaget in his attempted formalization of his theory of intelligence – are not adequate to express and distinguish between computational processes, so cannot adequately model the procedural aspect of knowledge.

In his discussions of cybernetics, Piaget sometimes refers approvingly to what he calls 'artificial intelligence'. For example, he says that 'in many respects life works like a cybernetic machine, an "artificial" or "general" intelligence', [S 114] and that 'one of the most instructive methods for analysing [the epistemic subject's] actions is to construct, by means of machines or equations, models of "artificial intelligence" for which a cybernetic theory can then furnish the necessary and sufficient conditions; what is being modelled in this way is not its structure in the abstract (algebra would suffice for this), but its effective realization and operation.' [S 69] The references to 'equations' and 'algebra' in this passage betray the fact that Piaget is not here thinking of AI as defined above. For we have seen that this offspring of cybernetics cannot be understood in the quantitative mathematical terms suited to its parent.

However, in 1960 Piaget said approvingly of the programming approach to psychology, 'I wish to urge that we make an attempt to use it.' [RB] He himself does not (although some Piagetians do), but he probably would have done so had he not already been an old man when it appeared. This is so not merely because AI is a development of cybernetics, which Piaget identifies as the general science of equilibration, but for four more specific reasons also.

First, AI precisely formalizes the phenomena it models, and, as we saw in Chapter 4, Piaget's logicist bias has led him to try to express his theory in precise formal (algebraic) terms. In biology too, Piaget's logicism leads him to praise attempts (like J. H. Woodger's) to supply 'a logistic axiomatization' of biological processes, and to commend d'Arcy Thompson for his geometrical approach to morphology. [BK 59 & 166] Piaget hopes to see a mathematized biological theory or 'organization mathematics', a theory that 'will have to take the form of some qualitative [*sic*] algebra, like that concerned with networks and groups, making allowance for the dynamism which is an essential part of all regulatory systems.' [BK 166-7]

Algebraic cybernetics, concerned essentially with quantitative measures, is used in some contexts by present-day biologists. But it is significant that C. H. Waddington (whose theory Piaget finds so congenial, and describes as 'inspired by cybernetics' [BK 66]) has recently agreed that 'the problems of biology are *all* to do with programs', that is, with 'lists of things to be done, with due regard to circumstances.'[5] Such problems, about what is to be done, focus on the very 'dynamism' of biological phenomena that Piaget wants a mathematical biology to illuminate. And it is programming or computational concepts (which the biologist B. C. Goodwin calls 'cognitive' concepts), not theories couched in the mathematical terms used by classical cybernetics, which are needed to express procedural matters such as these.

A second reason why Piaget's sympathetic response to the use of programming concepts in psychology is unsurprising is his intuition of the usefulness of mechanical working models of the mind (like Grey Walter's tortoises). He points out, in the passage cited earlier, that these represent 'not [only] its structure in the abstract . . .

but its effective realization and operation.' Interpreted in AI terms, this remark notes the two great advantages of a programming methodology.

A functioning program decisively tests the effectiveness of the programmed theory actually to generate the results it claims to imply (though whether the theory is an adequate reflection at any level of the way equivalent results are produced in human thinking is another question, requiring empirical investigation as in the case of any other psychological theory). In addition, so that the program will actually do something when it is run on a computer, the programmer must explicitly specify all the symbol-manipulation procedures whereby one informational structure or representation is transformed into or compared with another – which means that the programmed theory must detail the processes (as well as the organized data-structures) of thought. Since Piaget himself says that 'what is important for psychological explication is not equilibrium as a state but, rather, the actual process of equilibration', [6PS 101] without being clear as to the nature of this process, this second advantage of the present-day successors of Grey Walter's tortoises might be especially helpful in filling theoretical lacunae within his psychology.

Third, Piaget's structuralist philosophy of science is consonant with AI. An AI program does not provide detailed predictions of specific performances (it is usually impossible to predict precisely what a complex self-regulating program will do), and testing its explanatory power is not the same thing as testing its predictive power – positivist philosophies of science to the contrary.[6] Nor does it relate measurable parameters to quantitative laws which, as Piaget points out, is the ideal of classical physics – and of behaviourist psychology. [S 37-8] Rather, it expresses and integrates a range of structural possibilities, and thereby makes them systematically intelligible. The program is a finite set of rules with infinite generative power, and each of the differing instances to which it can give rise according to circumstance is explained by showing how it can be generated by the rule-system. This tallies with Piaget's description of a structuralist explanation as one in which 'the actual is now interpreted or explained as an instance of the possible', [S 38] while also illuminating why *this* possibility was actualized rather than *that*, and *how*. And psychologists and biologists influenced by the AI approach would endorse his essentially structuralist remark that 'An organism is a machine engaged in transformations.' [MI 8] Moreover, AI endorses Piaget's broadly Kantian view that empiricism must be replaced by a dynamic structuralism in psychology and epistemology. The computational prerequisite of learning, for instance, is an active system of information-processing structures that can construct, analyse, compare, select and otherwise manipulate varied information in increasingly adequate (equilibrated) ways. For the sorts of reasons given by Piaget, the empiricist alternative does not make computational sense.

Fourth and finally, Piaget's conception of the subject-matter of psychology is the same as that of those (increasingly numerous) cognitive psychologists who adopt a computational approach.[7] He defines psychology as being about 'mind' (not behaviour), [6PS 114] and rightly contrasts it with physiology by saying that psychology is concerned with 'systems of signification' inter-related by 'implication'. [MP xxiii] It is noteworthy that Piaget, the most 'biological' of psychologists, says relatively little about cerebral physiology. He is not concerned with the detailed material mechanisms of thinking (or, likewise, of embryological morphogenesis), so much as with its abstract logical structure.

Similarly, AI offers psychologists a way of theorizing about the inferential and representational aspects of thought, not its material base. Even computer simulations of neural nets, and McCulloch and Pitts's paper that so

impressed Piaget, take heed of neurophysiology only insofar as it seems relevant to the abstract logical properties
of neurones. Much as 'feedback' is an abstract cybernetic
notion that can be discussed apart from its embodiment
in any particular material system (which is why Piaget
could hope that it might provide a truly general theory of
equilibration), so programming concepts do not concern
the machinery of the computer. Piaget's anti-reductionist
view of psychology as a semiotic science of implication,
rather than a causal science of mechanism, is thus essentially compatible with the AI approach.

For these four reasons – his logicism, his approval of
functioning machine-models, his structuralism, and his
semiotic mentalism – Piaget's recommendation of the programming methodology is a natural development of his
commitment to the cybernetics from which AI has
evolved. It would be interesting to know what use he
would have made of it had he followed his own recommendation. As recently as 1975, he has tried to explain
the inner dynamics of equilibration in terms of different
types of 'disturbances', 'compensations' and 'regulations'
(including 'regulations of regulations') constituting 'positive
and negative feedback'. [DT] He suggests a number of important distinctions that could be much more clearly made
(and fruitfully elaborated) in computational terms. For
instance, consider his description of the bicycle rider: 'As
for outside obstacles, these are avoided, which means compensating for the disturbances by a whole or partial negation, the latter corresponding to a differentiation of the
scheme into sub-schemes which determine whether or not
the goal can be attained by a direct itinerary.' [DT 26]
Anyone familiar with AI work on planning – with its rich
distinctions between procedures for generating, evaluating, ordering and flexibly executing subgoals on hierarchical levels in the service of some overall goal – will
know how it could improve upon Piaget's vague account
of 'partial negation' in goal-seeking behaviour.[8] In short,

since computational concepts are specifically designed to analyse what in Piagetian terms one could call 'the dialectics of feedback in systems of signification based on implication', they may help in the detailed exploration of the equilibratory processes of the mind.

In his account of the continuous process of conceptual equilibration, Piaget faces questions analogous to those facing anyone who tries to model concept-learning in computational terms. For instance, consider his account of sensorimotor experience as enabling the baby to learn that *what-happens-after-I-move-my-hand* – or, more generally, *what-happens-after-what* – is an aspect of her world that is highly salient for successful motor action, and essential to the concept of *cause* that she gradually constructs. In order to learn such matters, she must possess computational mechanisms capable, among other things, of making the comparison underlying the perception of *what-happens-after-I-move*, and of generalizing this comparison over many different but analogous cases. As Piaget himself suggests, the baby needs rich computational structures or ways of organizing knowledge in order to acquire concepts like *cause* – or even notions like *movehand-makes-rattlemove*. (In Kantian terms, the forms of intuition must be rich enough to generate causal notions; though Kant of course ignored the development of the categories.) Human perceptions of conceptual salience, and the mental comparisons by way of which salient features are used in constructing new concepts, are often taken for granted by theoretical psychologists – but Piaget tries to make them explicit so as to account for conceptual development.

Issues of salience and comparison must be made wholly explicit in a computational model of concept learning, if the model is to be programmable. Some relevant issues have been raised in a recent discussion by P. H. Winston, asking how a program might learn to recognize an indefinite number of *arches* (for instance), not merely those exactly like the ones encountered in the learning sequence.[9] In Piagetian terms, how might it assimilate a varied range of individual inputs to one general schema, which consists of many co-ordinated sub-schemas, and how accommodate its schema to environmental features that do not fit its current conceptual construct? As the equilibratory heart of such a program, Winston suggests a number of comparison procedures, which assess the match or mismatch between the input (whether example or counterexample) and the current state of the developing concept. These would classify mismatches (what for Piaget are 'disturbances') into twenty-one distinct logical types, which differentially determine the nature of the accommodatory transformation of the concept's logical structure. Winston's program embodies some of these comparisons, but its assumptions about the possible dimensions of salience that it should attend to are much less rich than an adult's, or even an infant's. It is partly because of this that its concept of *arch* is considerably simpler than what a human subject understands by that term (and because of this also that its limited learning ability is not generalizable). But the program, and the programmer's discussion of how it might be improved, helps sensitize one to the sorts of question that would have to be answered by an adequate theory of equilibration. And it bears out Piaget's criticisms of empiricist theories of learning: to be able to make active use of an item of information (the presence or absence of a salient feature), it needs a computationally complex structure in terms of which to make logically subtle comparisons and effect appropriate transformations to the concept it is constructing.

It has been argued that this computational necessity, which goes against empiricist epistemologies, casts doubt on Piaget's attribution of stage-to-stage progression to processes of assimilation and accommodation like those involved in concept-learning.[10] The reason is that Piaget insists on a radical reconstruction (as opposed to an extension) of intellectual structures at each stage: the pre-

operational child, he says, is structurally incapable of understanding matters that will seem like child's play to her
later; and similar claims are made at the biological level,
so that the worm's knowledge is not equivalent to a tiny
part of ours but is something different out of which ours
has been reconstructed.

Briefly, the anti-Piagetian argument here is that any
computational mechanism (program or person) capable of
learning a new concept C must already be in possession of
a language with representational power rich enough to
express the content of C. C may be a concept expressible
in English or French, but at base there must be a language
of thought (what Piaget would term a system of 'significations') that underlies all natural languages and symbolic
systems, in which the content of C is in principle expressible. Certainly, C may be useful, or even in practice
necessary, as a shorthand expression making for ease
of thought, or computational efficiency. But if Piaget's
claim is to be accepted that the cognitive structures of
stage n are strictly incapable of expressing matters expressed by the later structures of stage $n+1$, then the progression from stage to stage cannot be explained in terms
of the sort of equilibratory processes assumed to underlie
the development of the *grasping* or *toy* (or *arch*) schemata.
In short, equilibration within a stage must be radically
different from equilibration between stages, which latter
should perhaps not be described in terms of equilibration
at all.

Piaget's concept of equilibration is not sufficiently clear
to settle these controversial computational issues, but
consideration of them might help in the clarification of
Piagetian theory that is needed. The Piagetian distinction
between *learning* and *development* might be adduced as
relevant here; but then the point is that development is an
even more mysterious process than learning, and indis-
criminate use of the term 'equilibration' misleadingly gives
the impression that processes capable of improving the

baby's grasping scheme (for example) are likewise capable of reconstructing sensorimotor into pre-operational stages of grasping.

Piaget relates the development of concepts to that of skills. 'HACKER' is an AI program with features comparable to some aspects of the learning of motor skills.[11] It learns how to plan the assembly of stacks of bricks (of which, like a baby, it can pick up only one at a time) because it can profit intelligently from its mistakes. Knowledge initially stored as factual data becomes accessible as practical know-how, which enables the program actively to restructure its representations of its tasks so as to carry them out more effectively. For example, the knowledge that a brick cannot be picked up if another brick is sitting on top of it is transformed by experience into the realization that the top blocks in a stack must be removed before any attempt is made to pick up the bottom one. This passage from 'mere knowledge' to 'practical understanding' is reminiscent of Piaget's distinction between *figurative* and *operative* knowing. Piaget suggests that this distinction has no significance at the sensorimotor stage, when perception and action are inextricably linked. But the computational difference between possessing a certain datum of knowledge and being able to use it in a structured activity is applicable to sensorimotor no less than operational knowing.

Two features of HACKER are especially important here. First, it classifies its failures in terms of five structurally distinct sorts of mistake, or 'bug', and transforms its action-schemas accordingly. That is, its mistakes act as specifically structured disequilibrating factors that initiate and guide appropriate accommodatory processes. Its mistakes are not simply *wrong*, but are (inadequate) first attempts at mastery of its problems. Second, it uses its representation of the goal (or sub-goal) in accessing, selecting and suitably transforming its block-moving routines.

We may compare these (rigorously formalized) abilities

with Piaget's (less well-specified) descriptions of the developing consciousness of action in pre-operational and concrete operational children, and of the intuitive invention of means by the Stage 6 sensorimotor baby. Children aged between four and twelve can do or attempt many motor-tasks (walking on all fours, using a lever or a catapult, seriating sticks) without knowing how they do so, and so without being able in many cases to correct their failures. Piaget says that consciousness 'proceeds from the periphery to the centre', since deliberate action first involves cognizance only of the goal pursued and the achieved success or failure, 'while the fact that the scheme that assigns a goal to the action immediately triggers off the means of effecting it (regardless of how appropriate these may be) may remain unconscious.' Later, largely because of the child's search for the reasons underlying her mistakes (*cf.* bugs), consciousness 'moves in the direction of the central regions of the action in order to reach its internal mechanism: recognition of the means employed, reasons for their selection or their modification en route, and the like.' [GC 334] An analysis of the self-monitoring behaviours reported by Piaget which used computational concepts such as those embodied in HACKER (and others yet to be developed) might clarify his account of the development of purposive self-knowledge in the pre-operational and concrete operational stage. Similarly, current and future computational concepts could help specify (which Piaget does not do) the *various* psychological functions that might be ascribed to a baby's opening her mouth in this sort of case:

Lucienne opens and closes her mouth while examining the slit of the box, proving that she is in the act of assimilating it and of mentally trying out the enlargement of the slit; moreover the analogy thus established by assimilation between the slit perceived and other openings simply evoked leads her to foresee that pressure put on the edge of the opening will widen it. Once the schemata have been thus spontaneously accommodated on the plane of simple mental assimilation, Lucienne proceeds to act and succeeds right away. [OIC 344]

Since HACKER is not a robot with a material hand, but a program that speculates on how such a robot should use its hand to achieve its goals, it cannot take advantage of the many unforeseen mismatches between plan and reality that arise in actual bodily movement: it merely simulates a limited class of these 'execution bugs'. Such mismatches are, however, available in profusion to the exploring baby, and to the five- or twelve-year-old puzzling over catapults. And Piaget often refers to the child's dialectical capitalization on happy accidents, such as the motion of a string touched by a baby's hand. But computational questions remain as to how the child recognizes the mismatch or the serendipity, and what computational resources she uses to profit from it. HACKER has a set of plan-CRITICS that enable the program to profit from some unforeseen events. For instance, they can recognize HACKER's moving a block from B to C having earlier moved it from A to B; they then advise HACKER to move the block directly from A to C in future, in like cases; as a result, HACKER formulates its block-moving plans more sensibly. But the program does not have enough intelligence (it lacks the necessary computational structures) to notice or profit from other happenings which may be of use to humans. Piaget's careful observations of babies and of older children (including their growing awareness of what they are doing and how they are doing it) help suggest what experiences are usefully assimilable by the child, but the details of the underlying computations are still unclear.

Some Piagetians claim that the notion of 'bug' that is used by HACKER, and by programmers generally, is a powerful idea in understanding how children learn.[12] They are experimenting with educational methods wherein the child learns about general structures of thinking – and general types of bug, or mistake – through the experience of writing simple computer programs whose effects (in making a mechanical 'turtle' move, in drawing pictures on a video-unit, or in producing music) are immediately apparent. Preliminary work with LOGO, a specially designed programming language, suggests that remedial mathematics (for example) is more easily assimilated by children whose insight into their own reasoning has been deepened by their experience of self-correctively constructing LOGO programs. In general, their activities using LOGO seem to help the children's consciousness to proceed 'from the periphery to the centre', and encourage the development of general problem-solving strategies as opposed to ungeneralizable *ad hoc* tricks useful only within a narrow domain. In varied areas of thinking, their attitude to their mistakes is radically changed: they come to see them as first steps in the construction of a solution, as opposed to mere stupid irrelevancies. This accords with Piaget's account of the growth of knowledge: the young child is not so much *wrong* about conservation, or cause, as unable fully to understand the structural possibilities appreciated by the adults. Improvement occurs through constructive self-correction (accommodation) on the child's part, and 'good' teaching encourages this autonomous process rather than inhibiting it by attempting to substitute another (less spontaneous) type of learning.

Perhaps surprisingly, some work in AI reinforces the criticism of Piaget made in Chapter 4, that he is overly 'logical' in his approach to intelligence. AI has recently been influenced by the idea that much of our knowledge is represented in organized stereotypes, schemas (*sic*), or 'frames', which include not only concrete content or data but also specific advice about what questions to ask about unspecified facts and what inferences to draw in particular circumstances. For example, if one is told that Mary is speaking to a waitress, one should normally infer that Mary is in a restaurant, and that she will soon order, eat and pay for food. But this is not a *deductive* inference: Mary may not be in a restaurant at all, and even if she is she may not order or eat or pay for anything (what if the food is ill-cooked, or the menu unsuitable?). Still less are one's commonsense inferences about Mary based in a combinatorial search through all the possibilities of what she might or might not do. Presumably, the reason for the rise from 19.3-per-cent success on the abstract logical task described in Chapter 4 to the 98-per-cent success in the more realistic situation lies in the fact that the latter subjects were somehow able to access their everyday knowledge, or 'postal frame', so as to solve the problem more quickly and more reliably than in the abstract case. Piaget seems comparable rather to the early 'theorem-proving' tradition in AI, whose proponents assumed that all problems could be solved by the use of very general methods of logical reasoning.

In addition to his 'Kantian' remarks about structures, Piaget also suggests pertinent questions and computationally interesting hypotheses about process. Some of these are currently being explored by Piagetians working in explicitly computational terms. For instance, Piaget explains the young child's inability fully to understand class inclusion by saying, 'If he thinks of the part A, the whole B ceases to be conserved as a unit, and the part A is henceforth comparable only to its complementary A'.' [PC 103] A study of Piagetian class-inclusion problems written within the AI paradigm discusses in detail many distinct procedural features of such problems.[18] For example, it clearly sets out the computational advantages of creating a *copy* of a mixed-item list before trying to count the items of a given type on the list. We may compare this with Piaget's explanation just cited, and with his remark about children apparently unable to handle class inclusion, 'They are unable to compare one of these parts with the whole, *which they have mentally destroyed*; they can compare only the two parts.' [6PS 53]

I say 'apparently' here, because recent work with six-year-olds shows that they can sometimes handle class-inclusion problems. One factor that helps them is the inclusion of a word in the test-question that emphasizes the class as a whole. Thus a child shown four toy cows (three black and one white) all lying 'sleeping' on their sides, is much more likely to answer correctly if she is asked *not*, 'Are there more black cows or more cows?' as in Piaget's standard form of question, but rather, 'Are there more black cows or more sleeping cows?'[14] The experimenter suggests that this helps prevent a failure of communication about what is required of the child (as can happen even when adults are posed similar questions) that is due to the artificiality of the standard class-inclusion question; certainly. 'Are there more black cows or more cows?' is a very unnatural query. But precisely how does it prevent misinterpretation, and precisely how does it also help the child to compare sub-class with class, rather than with the other sub-class (the white cow)? Evidently, the adjective 'sleeping' somehow helps the child to construct, retain, or otherwise manipulate the mixed-item list representing the whole class. It is the computational details which must differ between the two test-situations, which in abstract logical terms are equivalent (they both deal with class inclusion). Theoretical analysis of this detail, similar to the computational discussion cited in the previous paragraph, might help to clarify a wide range of differing behaviours on 'class-inclusion' problems.

A recent study aiming in this way to unify a superficially chaotic variety of individual cases, without losing sight of the idiosyncratic details, is R. M. Young's work on the development of seriation.[15] Starting from Piaget's observations of the three stages of seriation (see Chapter 4), Young ends by rejecting Piaget's theory of stage-discontinuity. Young describes different seriation behaviours by differing sets of information-processing rules. Because the addition of only one rule is often equivalent to an overall qualitative change in observed behaviour, Young concludes that psychological development is not holistically organized and discontinuous, but is an incremental process involving the learning of many 'surprisingly independent' rules. With regard to the Stage III child's (or adult's) seemingly illogical tendency to use Stage II trial-and-error seriation when presented with a large number of blocks with which to construct a staircase, Young criticizes Piaget for interpreting this as 'regression' to a pre-operational structure not optimally suited to the problem. Rather, he says, such behaviour shows the older child's flexibility in picking the most appropriate item from a repertoire of separable rules. For with a large number of blocks, even the adult cannot perceive which is the longest, and so cannot reliably pick it out as would be required by the fully 'operational' seriation-strategy.

Each rule is a Condition-Action pair, specifying a Condition (a state of the environment or of the thinking going on) whose presence triggers the relevant action (a bodily or mental action). Two examples are, 'IF you want to add a block to the staircase THEN decide that you want to get a suitable one from the pool, that is, one of about the right size,' and 'IF you want to place a block in the staircase, and there are just two blocks in it already, similar in size but the wrong way round THEN rotate the two blocks.'

Young combines his AI approach with an experimental methodology, trying to match his rule-systems to individual children. As well as distinguishing the broad behavioural differences that typify Piaget's three stages (being able or unable to build or make insertions into a staircase), Young notes finer details – such as the child's choice of one specific block rather than another, the movement of the hand toward a block that is not in fact picked up, and the child's *double* tapping of a block which is two units smaller than its neighbour when the child's finger is 'running down the staircase'. In terms of the selection, evaluation and placement of blocks, he defines a three-dimensional 'space' of seriation skills. A child's location within this structuralist space characterizes the problems she can and cannot solve, and the nature of her errors; distinctive types of seriation behaviour are associated with different regions of the space. As a general methodological moral, he concludes that Piagetians (and other psychologists) should pay more attention than is usual to such detailed computational questions as *What* information is the subject using? *When* does she pick it up? *How* does she obtain it? and *What* does she use it for?

It is not clear that Young's critique of Piagetian theory is entirely in order. One might reply, for instance, that Piaget is interested in general competence rather than specific performance, and that questions such as those just listed concern the latter. Moreover, Piaget claims to have identified the simultaneous appearance of certain logical structures in behaviour in varied domains, and that it is this generality which requires theoretical explanation (and which justifies the conception of *stages* in mental development). For example, Piaget reports that children come to manage tactile seriation at about the same age as visual seriation. [EGL 261] Young does discuss the generalization of seriation from blocks to discs; but he has not shown that he could write a set of rules to cover visual and tactile seriation, or to express seriation in such abstract terms that it could straight away be incorporated into a theory of the development of *number*, as Piagetian theory would require. Again, Young's claim to have explained the theoretically perplexing phenomenon of *horizontal décalage* between length and weight seriation may be to the point: but his (experimentally supported) belief that décalage is due to perceptual constraints, since one cannot simply see or feel whether identically sized blocks are equal in weight, is seemingly anticipated by

Piaget's reference to the child's 'perceptual adjustment to an intuitive whole'. [EGL 251] In addition, many computationally-minded psychologists would reject Young's 'Condition-Action Rules' approach, preferring alternative AI methodologies of a more hierarchically structured type – whether concerned with Piaget's theories or anyone else's.

The point of general importance, however, is that computational ideas about informational feedback in symbol-manipulating systems can help to suggest detailed elaborations and criticisms of Piaget's theory. They can aid in the planning of empirical studies and the interpretation of experimental results, by sensitizing psychologists to the many distinct computational functions that might underlie a given observation. This is true even though the current achievements of AI fall short of its future promise, and far short of the complexities of the human mind.[16]

Finally, computational concepts can help counter the charge that Piaget's concept of equilibrium is mere 'surplus baggage' by focusing on and further specifying his many insightful remarks about the psychological mechanisms of equilibration. Interpreted in computational (rather than quantitative or algebraic) terms, 'equilibration' is a useful concept like the similarly general 'feedback' (of which according to Piaget it is a virtual synonym). Computational ideas have evolved partly from the cybernetics that Piaget has championed so strongly, and they are philosophically in accord with his formalist psychological structuralism. Like Piagetian theory, but with more detailed success, programming concepts are concerned with the dynamic processes of the use of knowledge and the development of cognitive structures.

It is no wonder, then, that Piaget has urged psychologists to make an attempt to use such concepts. In the late 1960s (by which time he was already over seventy) he replied to a query about the possible relevance of AI to his theory that he believed it might be helpful, and 'wished strongly' that the approach should be explored; likewise, he said that these techniques of computer simulation promised to be 'the most decisive for the study of structures'.[17] The Piagetians (and other cognitive psychologists) who are currently using this methodology may justifiably be even more hopeful today than Piaget was in 1947, before the fledgling cybernetics had given rise to AI, when he remarked, 'the psychological theory of intellectual mechanisms is only in its infancy, and we are barely beginning to glimpse the sort of precision of which it might be capable.' [PI v]

8　How Important is Piaget?

The question *How important is Piaget?* can be interpreted
in several ways. First, as a matter of intellectual history:
Has he been influential? The answer to this question depends less on what he said than on what he was generally
believed to have said, and not at all on whether what he
said was right. Second, a question whose answer will
decide whether one regards his influence as unfortunate
or benign: *Were his views more nearly correct than those
of his contemporaries?* Third, a question situated in one's
own historical stage of understanding rather than his, the
answer to which in principle could differ from the answer
giver to the previous question: *Was he correct?* And
fourth, a question about his current rather than his
historical importance: *Should someone starting from
scratch today be advised to read him for his lasting intellectual contribution to psychology?*

The answers to these four questions are respectively,
Yes, very; Yes; Yes and no; and *Yes, but . . .* These answers
and their qualifications are implicit in the previous chapters, but it may be useful in conclusion to make them
explicit so that the strengths and weaknesses of Piaget's
work can be summarized and compared.

Piaget's influence in psychology has been enormous,
especially in his later years, by which time American experimental psychology had moved toward a philosophical
base more congruent with his approach than was the
positivistic behaviourism of the first half of the century.
Granted, there is an increasingly influential school of
'ecological' psychologists who see the newborn baby (and
the adult) as engaged in perceptual discovery of the world
rather than intellectual construction of it.[1] But they

typically acknowledge Piaget as their most important theoretical adversary, and fully endorse his emphasis on inherited biological structures or mechanisms affording the basis of our knowledge. The epigenetic aspects of Piaget's psychology are not always recognized by people not well acquainted with his writings. So he is sometimes believed to have said that the developmental stages are preformed and unfolded by maturation, or triggered by environmental conditions, instead of emerging through a dialectical interaction with the child's world. Educational programmes (for instance) based on either of these misconceptions may truly claim to be inspired by Piaget, but rest on a misunderstanding of his position.

In biology Piaget's influence has been minimal, understandably so. For his unorthodox views were expressed with insufficient clarity to command attention from theoretical biologists, while also making unacceptable biological claims. Even C. H. Waddington, with whose epigenetic biology Piaget has most sympathy, rejects crucial Piagetian claims (such as the biological inevitability of the evolution of logic). However, in its broad outlines Piaget's approach is consonant with some significant developments in modern biology.

In philosophy, too, Piaget's work has not received the recognition he hoped for (though more philosophers than biologists read him). This is due less to the many unclarities and logical mistakes in his writings than to the common philosophical doctrine that theoretical psychology as an empirically based discipline can have no relevance to purely philosophical, epistemological questions. If one believes, with Piaget, that there can be no such clearcut separation of psychological from epistemological questions, one may regret that his philosophical influence has not been greater. He is firmly situated in a continuing philosophical tradition, within which his closest intellectual companion is Kant. But much as Kant was speaking to the empiricist Hume, Piaget is speaking to the nativist Kant, urging a concentration on developmental issues which in Kantian epistemology were ignored.

Throughout his early and middle years, Piaget's main psychological contemporaries were the behaviourists, Gestaltists and Freudians. With hindsight one can say that the questions he was asking, and the answers he was giving, were much deeper and more fruitful than those of behaviourist learning-theory. His ideas of psychological structure, of mental operations and cognitive transformations, and of innate cognitive principles whereby the baby organizes and learns from her experience were all important, and radically opposed to behaviourist theory. The Gestaltists and Freudians both shared his concern with mental structure, and agreed with him that psychological theory must take account of non-introspectible mental processes. But the Gestaltists ignored problems of cognitive development, while the Freudians (who focused on developmental issues) paid more attention to emotional and motivational phenomena than to cognition. However, Freud said more of relevance to cognitive psychology than Piaget to psychodynamics, even though Piaget does make a place for motivation and emotion in his overall theoretical system.[2]

This last point is often raised in present-day assessments of Piaget, who is commonly accused of ignoring the social and motivational dimensions of the mind. To some degree such criticism is misplaced, for no one person can do everything and it is defensible to decide that one will concentrate on cognitive rather than motivational phenomena. Up to a point, the same could be said of individual as opposed to social aspects of psychology. But there comes a point at which the study of cognition, or knowledge, demands attention to social factors. For instance, the personal interactions between mother and baby prior to and during the baby's acquisition of language have only recently become the focus of developmental research, and the current questions about their function in cognitive organization have not arisen out of a specifically Piagetian approach. Even more important, the social phenomenon of language (both within and outside educational institutions) is closely related to knowledge, and one might expect that a cognitive psychologist would pay a good deal of attention to it. However, with the exception of his early work on egocentric speech (which is now generally agreed to be largely mistaken), Piaget has not studied language closely. Piagetians of course believe that the basic organizing principles of knowledge arise prior to language, and that logic structures language rather than vice versa. And they have done research (for example into the cognitive development of deaf children) related to this theoretical claim. But bearing in mind the enormous range and amount of Piaget's research, it is surprising that more attention was not given to language as a cognitive phenomenon, despite Piaget's theoretical position with regard to it. Even were its social nature to be underplayed, the importance of language as a cognitive influence within the individual (or epistemic subject) might have been more fully recognized.

Recent experimental research has shown Piaget to be wrong on many points, such as the inability of children at a given age to carry out certain types of 'more advanced' thinking, or precursors thereof (such as the perceptually mediated transitive inferences reported by P. Bryant). And adults, by contrast, are considerably less logical in much of their reasoning than Piaget's theory would lead one to expect. This illogicality is not mere sloppiness or error, but is essential to an intelligence functioning within a complex and rapidly changing world. It is therefore of epistemological as well as psychological importance. The stage-concept has become increasingly dubious, and many present-day psychologists would deny the existence of a distinct type of sensorimotor intelligence, whose principles are radically different from the intelligence of the young child. But one should not forget that many of these experiments (including those able to take advantage of very recent techniques) would not have been carried out were it not for Piaget's seminal claims. Science has been described as a process of conjectures and refutations – and someone has to make the conjecture before anyone can provide the refutation.

A drawback more important than his errors on specific points is Piaget's general failure to appreciate the possibility of alternative theoretical explanations, and to plan his experiments carefully enough to exclude them. Too often, even in his later research, Piaget relies on evidence so informally presented as to be almost anecdotal in character. Thus Bryant, for instance, disputes neither Piaget's observations nor their consistency with Piaget's theory; but he does dispute the claim that only Piaget's theory can account for them. Moreover, he believes that his painstaking experiments, involving carefully planned experimental controls, support his own theoretical position and show Piaget's to be radically false. Whether or not one accepts Bryant's case, one may wish that the conceptual relations between Piaget's experiments and his theory were rather tighter.

It is partly because these relations are not tighter that it is often possible to amend Piaget's claims so as to take account of new, apparently conflicting, evidence. But this possibility may sometimes seem too strong for comfort, suggesting that his theory is so vague as to be virtually unfalsifiable. For example, his claim that limbless babies of normal intelligence present no essential challenge to his views on sensorimotor development threatens to rescue his theory only by depriving it of its content. Even so, it is undeniable that his theoretical account of sensorimotor development has been a powerful heuristic in formulating psychological questions and encouraging empirical research in this area.

It is in the latter sense, too, that I have argued for the heuristic force of his admittedly vague notion of equilibrium. He has used this notion to unify a diverse range of psychological (and biological) questions, and to encourage psychologists to look for reciprocal and self-regulating processes of adjustment to and modification of the (external and internal) environment within every psychological phenomenon. In general terms, he identified this psychological self-regulation with cybernetic feedback, which we have seen to be inadequate in its traditional sense to express the processes concerned. 'Feedback', or 'equilibrium', needs to be extended – some would say replaced – by information-processing concepts that have recently entered cognitive psychology from the context of artificial intelligence and the theory of computation.

The computational approach is an increasingly influential though still controversial force in current psychology, and one with which Piaget has expressed sympathy on several occasions. Looked at from this viewpoint, Piaget's theory is praiseworthy for its 'Kantian' stress on self-organizing mental structures and cognitive transformations, and for its insistence on the underlying complexities of everyday (even infantile) psychological phenomena that are introspectively simple. But the actual psychological (information-processing) complexity must be greater still, and its expression – which remains to be achieved – will require concepts that Piaget himself does not use (though some Piagetians do). That is, it will require detailed computational concepts in terms of which theory and experiment can be formulated, planned and assessed. However, since these are of very recent origin (and in their current stage of development are still painfully inadequate to the richness of the mind), it would be anachronistic to chide Piaget – already eighty-three years old – for not having used them himself. What is more to the point is that his cybernetic interpretation of equilibrium (as well as his formalist focus on the implicational structures within the mind) was basically in accord with this more recent – and potentially more fruitful – approach.

In sum, despite all the criticisms, there is a rich store of psychological insights and theoretical speculations, and a profusion of intriguing empirical observations and remarkably ingenious experiments, to be found in Piaget's pioneering work. Educational, developmental and cognitive psychology are all informed by his thought. And for those interested in the broader context of psychology, he raises important and still unresolved questions about the relation between individual sciences (such as biology and psychology), between science and philosophy, and between knowledge and wisdom. Even those who believe (in my view, wrongly) that scientific and philosophical questions can be sharply separated, can gain epistemological illumination from his account of the growth of children's knowledge of space, time, cause and objectivity – for much of what he has to say may help in the conceptual analysis of philosophically basic concepts such as these. So to someone attracted today to psychological or epistemological enquiry, one may say: 'Read Piaget. Remember that he is usually vague and often wrong, and that there are still-uncharted dimensions of structural and procedural complexity within the mind that he seemingly has little inkling of. But yes – read Piaget.'

Notes

1. Piaget the Polymath

1. *American Psychologist*, 25 (1970), p. 65.
2. R. J. Evans, *Jean Piaget: the Man and His Ideas* (Dutton, 1973), p. 50.
3. B. Rotman, *Jean Piaget: Psychologist of the Real* (Harvester, 1977), Ch. 7.
4. J. H. Flavell, *The Developmental Psychology of Jean Piaget* (Van Nostrand, 1963).
5. J. S. Bruner, 'Inhelder and Piaget's *The Growth of Logical Thinking*', *British Journal of Psychology*, 50 (1959), p. 365.

2. The Intelligent Baby

1. R. W. White, 'Motivation Reconsidered: the Concept of Competence', *Psychological Review*, 66 (1959), 297-333; H. Helson, 'Adaptation-Level Theory', in S. Koch, ed., *Psychology, a Study of a Science*, Vol. I; *Sensory, Perceptual and Physiological Formulations* (McGraw Hill, 1959).
2. F. C. Bartlett, *Remembering: a Study in Experimental and Social Psychology* (Cambridge University Press, 1932).
3. G. A. Miller and P. N. Johnson-Laird, *Language and Perception* (Harvard University Press, 1976).
4. K. Nelson, 'Some Evidence for the Cognitive Primacy of Categorization and its Functional Basis', in P. N. Johnson-Laird and P. C. Wason, eds., *Thinking: Readings in Cognitive Science* (Cambridge University Press,

1977), pp. 223-38.

5. A. Sloman, *The Computer Revolution in Philosophy: Philosophy, Science, and Models of Mind* (Harvester, 1978), pp. 202-4.

6. R. S. Peters, *Ethics and Education* (Allen & Unwin, 1966), p. 229.

7. O. O. Kilpatrick, Comments on Piaget in *Journal of Research in Science Teaching*, 2 (1964), 247-51.

8. T. G. R. Bower, *A Primer of Infant Development* (Freeman, 1977).

9. P. C. Dodwell, D. Muir and D. Di Franco, 'Responses of Infants to Visually Presented Objects', *Science*, 194 (1976), pp. 209-11; H. McGurk, 'Visual Perception in Young Infants', in B. Foss, ed., *New Perspectives in Child Development* (Penguin, 1974), esp. pp. 45-7.

10. W. Stone, H. T. Smith and L. B. Murphy, eds., *The Competent Infant* (Tavistock, 1974).

11. N. Jordan, 'Is there an Achilles Heel in Piaget's Theorizing?', *Human Development*, 15 (1972), pp. 379-82.

12. C. B. Kopp and J. Shaperman, 'Cognitive Development in the Absence of Object Manipulation during Infancy', *Developmental Psychology*, 9 (1973), p. 430; five years later, one of the authors wrote to me: 'He is currently enrolled in private elementary school. Reports from the staff indicate he is meeting, or excelling in some areas, academic expectations.'

13. Letter written at Piaget's direction, quoted in paper cited in Note 11, above.

14. Piagetian letter, in paper cited in Note 11, above.

3. The Intuitive Child

1. B. B. Lloyd, *Perception and Cognition: a Cross-Cultural Perspective* (Penguin, 1972); N. Warren, 'Universality and Plasticity, Ontogeny and Phylogeny: the Resonance Between Culture and Cognitive Development', in H. J. Sants, ed., *Social Implications of Developmental Psychology* (Macmillan, in press).

2. J. S. Bruner, *Toward a Theory of Instruction* (Norton, 1968), p. 44.

3. H. G. Furth, *Thinking Goes to School: Piaget's Theory in Practice* (Oxford University Press, 1975).

4. H. G. Furth, *Piaget for Teachers* (Prentice Hall, 1970).

5. PC 87-9; and H. G. Furth, *Thinking without Language: Psychological Implications of Deafness* (Free Press, 1966).

6. R. F. Cromer, 'Conservation by the Congenitally Blind', *Brit. J. Psychology*, 64 (1973), pp. 241-50.

7. H. Sinclair, 'Sensorimotor Action Patterns as a Condition for the Acquisition of Syntax', in R. Huxley and E. Ingram, eds., *Language Acquisition: Models and Methods* (Academic Press, 1971).

8. M. A. Boden, 'Implications of Language Studies for Human Nature', in T. Simon, ed., *Language, Mind and Brain: Interdisciplinary Perspectives* (in press).

9. M. Donaldson, *Children's Minds* (Fontana, 1978), pp. 20-4.

10. *Ibid.*, pp. 19-25.

11. J. S. Bruner, 'The Ontogenesis of Speech Acts', *Journal of Child Language*, 2 (1975), pp. 1-19; J. S. Bruner, 'Learning How to Do Things with Words', in J. S. Bruner and A. Garton, eds., *Human Growth and Development* (Oxford University Press, 1978), pp. 62-84.

12. L. S. Vygotsky, *Thought and Language* (MIT Press, 1962). Piaget's *Comments on Vygotsky's Critical Re-*

marks was published as a pamphlet by MIT in 1962.

13. *Cf.* J. H. Flavell, *Cognitive Development* (Prentice Hall, 1977), pp. 220-31.

14. P. Bryant, *Perception and Understanding in Young Children*: *an Experimental Approach* (Methuen, 1974).

15. *Ibid.*, p. 9.

4. Logic in Action

1. J. S. Bruner, R. R. Olver and P. M. Greenfield, eds., *Studies in Cognitive Growth* (Wiley, 1966).

2. L. S. Vygotsky, *Thought and Language* (MIT Press, 1962).

3. S. R. Tulkin and M. J. Konner, 'Alternative Conceptions of Intellectual Functioning', *Human Development*, 16 (1973), pp. 33-52.

4. 'Piagetian' results are described by J. Smedslund, 'The Acquisition of Conservation of Substance and Weight in Children', *Scandinavian J. Psychology*, 2 (1961), pp. 11-20, 71-87, 153-60, 203-10. 'Anti-Piagetian' results are reported by C. J. Brainerd, 'Learning Research and Piagetian Theory', in L. S. Siegel and C. J. Brainerd, eds.. *Alternatives to Piaget*: *Critical Essays on the Theory* (Academic Press, 1978), pp. 69-110.

5. C. Parsons, 'Inhelder and Piaget's *The Growth of Logical Thinking*', *Brit. J. Psychology*, 51 (1960), p. 78.

6. P. C. Wason, 'The Theory of Formal Operations: a Critique', in B. A. Geber, ed., *Piaget and Knowing: Studies in Genetic Epistemology* (Routledge & Kegan Paul, 1977), pp. 119-35.

7. D. N. Osherson, *Logical Abilities in Children* (Erlbaum, 1974).

5. Piaget and Philosophy

1. N. Chomsky, *Cartesian Linguistics* (Harper & Row, 1966); N. Chomsky, *Language and Mind* (Harcourt Brace, 1968).

2. N. Malcolm, 'The Myth of Cognitive Processes and Structures', in T. Mischel, ed., *Cognitive Development and Epistemology* (Academic Press, 1971), pp. 385-92; cf. M. Martin, 'Are Cognitive Processes and Structures a Myth?', *Analysis*, 33 (1973), pp. 83-8.

3. G. E. Moore, 'The Refutation of Idealism', in his *Philosophical Studies* (Routledge & Kegan Paul, 1922), pp. 1-30.

4. For the argument that science – including Piagetian psychology – always rests on realist assumptions, see N. E. Wetherick's 'Comment' on C. J. Brainerd in 'The Stage Question in Cognitive-Developmental Theory', *Behavioural and Brain Sciences*, 2 (1978), esp. p. 205; and cf. R. Bhaskar, *A Realist Theory of Science* (Harvester, 1978).

5. D. W. Hamlyn, *Experience and the Growth of Understanding* (Routledge & Kegan Paul, 1978); A. Wilden, *System and Structure: Essays in Communication and Exchange* (Tavistock, 1972).

6. D. W. Hamlyn, 'Epistemology and Conceptual Development', in T. Mischel, ed., *Cognitive Development and Epistemology* (Academic Press, 1971), p. 5.

7. Hamlyn, 'Epistemology and Conceptual Development', p. 23.

8. B. Rotman, *Jean Piaget: Psychologist of the Real* (Harvester, 1977), Ch. 7.

9. I. Lakatos, *Proofs and Refutations* (Cambridge University Press, 1976).

10. K. Popper, *Conjectures and Refutations* (Routledge & Kegan Paul, 1963).

11. R. Edgley, *Reason in Theory and Practice* (Hutchinson, 1969).

12. See the three books cited in Notes 5 and 8 above. For a philosophically informed defence of Piaget, see W. Mays, 'Genetic Epistemology and Theories of Adaptive Behaviour', in N. Bolton, ed., *Philosophical Problems in Psychology* (Methuen, in press).

13. The social implications of sociobiology are explored by M. Midgley, *Beast and Man: the Roots of Human Nature* (Harvester, 1979).

6. Piaget and Biology

1. C. H. Waddington, *The Strategy of the Genes* (Allen & Unwin, 1957).

2. C. H. Waddington, 'The Practical Consequences of Metaphysical Beliefs on a Biologist's Work: an Autobiographical Note', in C. H. Waddington, ed., *Toward a Theoretical Biology*, 2: *Sketches* (Edinburgh University Press, 1969), pp. 79 and 75.

3. C. H. Waddington, *The Evolution of an Evolutionist* (Edinburgh University Press, 1975), p. 92.

4. J. Maynard-Smith, *The Theory of Evolution*, 3rd edn. (Penguin, 1975), pp. 303-10.

5. J. Maynard-Smith, 'The Status of Neo-Darwinism', in Waddington, ed., *Toward a Theoretical Biology*, 2, pp. 82-105. (Includes comments by Waddington and others.)

6. Waddington, ed., *Toward a Theoretical Biology*, 2, p. 114.

7. C. H. Waddington, *The Nature of Life* (Allen & Unwin, 1961).

8. B. C. Goodwin, *Analytical Physiology of Cells and Developing Organisms* (Academic Press, 1976), p. 223.

9. C. H. Waddington, 'Form ^nd Information', and 'Epilogue', in C. H. Waddington, ed., *Toward a Theor-*

etical Biology, 4: *Essays* (Edinburgh University Press, 1972), pp. 109-45 and 283-90.

10. Goodwin, *Analytical Physiology*, p. vi.

11. B. C. Goodwin, 'A Cognitive View of Biological Process', *Journal of Social Biological Structure*, 1 (1978), pp. 117-25.

12. Goodwin, *Analytical Physiology*, p. 225.

7. Piaget and Cybernetics

1. N. Wiener, in A. Rosenblueth, N. Wiener and J. Bigelow, 'Behavior, Purpose and Teleology', *Philosophy of Science*, 10 (1943), p. 19.

2. C. Bernard's *Introduction to Experimental Medicine* (1866) and *General Physiology* (1872) introduced the idea of the self-regulating 'internal environment', which was called *homeostasis* by W. B. Cannon in *The Wisdom of the Body* (Norton, 1932). Cybernetics was founded by N. Wiener, *Cybernetics, or Control and Communication in the Animal and the Machine* (Wiley, 1948). Other classic texts include: W. R. Ashby, *Design for a Brain: the Origin of Adaptive Behaviour* (Wiley, 1952); W. Grey Walter, *The Living Brain* (Duckworth, 1953); W. S. McCulloch and W. H. Pitts, 'A Logical Calculus of the Ideas Immanent in Nervous Activity', *Bulletin of Mathematical Biophysics*, 5 (1943), pp. 115-33; L. von Bertalanffy, *General System Theory: Foundations, Development, Applications* (Brazilier, 1968); T. Parsons and E. Shils, *Toward a General Theory of Action* (Harvard, 1951).

3. See ref. cited in Note 1, above.

4. For an account of AI which stresses its psychological relevance, see M. A. Boden, *Artificial Intelligence and Natural Man* (Harvester, 1977).

5. See Waddington's comments in C. H. Longuet-Higgins, 'What Biology Is About', in C. H. Waddington, ed.,

Toward a Theoretical Biology, 2: *Sketches* (Edinburgh University Press, 1969), pp. 227-35.

6. Cf. 'What Are the Aims of Science?', in A. Sloman, *The Computer Revolution in Philosophy*: *Philosophy, Science, and Models of Mind* (Harvester, 1978), Ch. 2.

7. References to cognitive psychologists taking a computational approach are given by Boden, *Artificial Intelligence and Natural Man*, esp. pp. 516-17.

8. See Boden, *Artificial Intelligence and Natural Man*, pp. 354-70.

9. P. H. Winston, 'Learning Structural Descriptions from Examples', in P. H. Winston, ed., *The Psychology of Computer Vision* (McGraw Hill, 1975), pp. 157-210.

10. J. A. Fodor, *The Language of Thought* (Harvester, 1976), pp. 86-95.

11. G. J. Sussman, *A Computer Model of Skill Acquisition* (Elsevier, 1975).

12. S. Papert, *Piagetian Learning in a Computer Culture* (Harvester, forthcoming).

13. D. Klahr and J. G. Wallace, 'Class Inclusion Processes', in S. Farnham-Diggory, ed., *Information Processing in Children* (Academic Press, 1972), pp. 144-72.

14. M. Donaldson, *Children's Minds* (Fontana, 1978), p. 44.

15. R. M. Young, *Seriation by Children: an Artificial Intelligence Analysis of a Piagetian Task* (Birkhausen, 1976).

16. Some limitations of current AI are discussed in Boden, *Artificial Intelligence and Natural Man*.

17. J. Piaget, *Les Modèles et la Formalisation du Comportement* (Editions du Centre National de la Recherche Scientifique, 1967), p. 318. The other quote ('Je le souhaite tres vivement') was in a Radio Canada TV interview of 1969, between Piaget and T. Gouin-Décarie (Jean Gascon, personal communication).

8.   How Important is Piaget?

1. J. J. Gibson, *An Ecological Approach to Visual Perception* (Houghton-Mifflin, 1978).
2. See P. A. Cowan, *Piaget with Feeling: Cognitive, Social and Emotional Dimensions* (Holt, Rinehart & Winston, 1978); for a criticism of Piaget's excessive 'cognitivism', see D. W. Hamlyn, *Experience and the Growth of Understanding* (Routledge & Kegan Paul, 1978).

Bibliography and Abbreviations

The following works by Piaget are cited in the text. They are listed here in chronological order. The first column gives the abbreviations I have used, the second gives the date of first publication, the third gives the date of English translation and the last gives the title and the publisher of the English edition. Since most of Piaget's books are published by Routledge and Kegan Paul I have used the briefer RKP for this publisher.

G	1915–18	1977	'The Mission of the Idea', 'Biology and War' and 'Recherche', all in H. E. Gruber and J. J. Vonèche, eds., *The Essential Piaget: An Interpretive Reference and Guide*, RKP.
LTC	1923	1926	*The Language and Thought of the Child*, RKP.
JRC	1924	1926	*Judgment and Reasoning in the Child*, RKP.
CCW	1926	1929	*The Child's Conception of the World*, RKP.
CCPC	1927	1960	*The Child's Conception of Physical Causality*, RKP.
MJC	1932	1932	*The Moral Judgment of the Child*, RKP.
CIC	1936	1952	*The Origins of Intelligence in the Child*, RKP.
CCR	1936	1954	*The Child's Construction of Reality*, RKP.

CCN	1941	1952	*The Child's Conception of Number*, RKP.
PDI	1946	1951	*Play, Dreams and Imitation in Childhood*, RKP.
CCT	1946	1969	*The Child's Conception of Time*, RKP.
CCMS	1946	1970	*The Child's Conception of Movement and Speed*, RKP.
PI	1947	1950	*The Psychology of Intelligence*, RKP.
CCS	1948	1956	*The Child's Conception of Space* (with B. Inhelder), RKP.
CCG	1948	1960	*The Child's Conception of Geometry* (with B. Inhelder and A. Szeminska), RKP.
IEG	1950	[—]	*Introduction a l'Epistémologie Génétique*, 3 vols., Presses Universitaires de France.
A	1952	[—]	'Autobiography', in E. G. Boring, ed., *A History of Psychology in Autobiography*, Vol. 4, pp. 237-56, New York: Russell & Russell.
LP	1953	[—]	*Logic and Psychology*, Manchester University Press.
GLT	1955	1958	*The Growth of Logical Thinking: From Childhood to Adolescence* (with B. Inhelder), RKP.
EGL	1959	1964	*The Early Growth of Logic in the Child* (with B. Inhelder), RKP.
RB	1960	[—]	'Reply', to J. S. Bruner, 'Individual and Collective Problems in the Study of Thinking', *Annals of New York Academy*

			of Science, 91 (1960), pp. 22-37.
MP	1961	1969	The Mechanisms of Perception, RKP.
FP	1963	1969	Experimental Psychology, Its Scope and Method, Vol. 7: Intelligence (eds. Paul Fraisse and J. Piaget), RKP.
6PS	1964 (but items from 1940)	1968	Six Psychological Studies, Harvester Press.
ME	1965	1966	Mathematical Epistemology and Psychology (with E. W. Beth), D. Reidel.
IIP	1965	1971	Insights and Illusions of Philosophy, RKP.
NS	1966	–	'Nécessité et Signification des Recherches Comparatives en Psychologie Génétique', International Journal of Psychology, 1 (1966), pp. 3-13.
BK	1967	1971	Biology and Knowledge, Edinburgh University Press.
S	1968	1971	Structuralism, RKP.
MI	1968	1973	Memory and Intelligence (with B. Inhelder), RKP.
H	1970	–	'Piaget's Theory', in P. H. Mussen, ed., Carmichael's Handbook of Child Psychology, pp. 703-32, Wiley.
GE	1970	–	Genetic Epistemology, Columbia University Press.
PGE	1970	1972	Principles of Genetic Epistemology, RKP.
IDR	1970	–	Main Trends in Interdisciplinary Research, Allen & Unwin.

HD	1972	⌐—⌐	'Intellectual Evolution from Adolescence to Adulthood', *Human Development*, 15 (1972), pp. 1-12.
GC	1974	1976	*The Grasp of Consciousness*, RKP.
DT	1975	1978	*The Development of Thought: Equilibration and Cognitive Structures*, Blackwell.
AP	1978	⌐—⌐	'What is Psychology?', *American Psychologist*, 33 (1978), pp. 648-52.

On Reading Piaget

A clear statement of Piaget's general position (written in 1940) is his essay 'The Mental Development of the Child', in 6PS. A later (1970), but more abstract, summary is his paper 'Piaget's Theory', in H. His autobiography (1952) appears in A. Entire, but short, books summarizing his work are PI, PC, GE and S. These are very abstract in nature, and his early books provide a better sense of his empirical examples (see Bibliography). A useful selection of his work, some of it translated for the first time, appears in G (900 pages), together with interpretive comments by the editors.

Of the many secondary sources, H. Ginsburg and S. Opper, *Piaget's Theory of Intellectual Development: an Introduction* (Prentice Hall, 1969) gives a summary and J. H. Flavell, *The Developmental Psychology of Jean Piaget* (Van Nostrand, 1963) provides a longer account of Piaget's work. Affective issues are stressed in P. A. Cowan, *Piaget, with Feeling: Cognitive, Social, and Emotional Dimensions* (Holt, Rinehart & Winston, 1978), and educational implications are explored in H. G. Furth, *Piaget for Teachers* (Prentice Hall, 1970) and D. W. McNally, *Piaget, Education, and Teaching* (Harvester, 1977).

There is no single alternative to Piagetian theory in developmental psychology, but different perspectives are seen in J. S. Bruner, R. R. Olver and P. M. Greenfield, eds., *Studies in Cognitive Growth* (Wiley, 1966), J. S. Bruner, *Beyond the Information Given* (Allen & Unwin, 1974); J. H. Flavell, *Cognitive Development* (Prentice Hall, 1977); T. G. R. Bower, *A Primer of Infant Development* (Freeman,

1977); and M. Donaldson, *Children's Minds* (Fontana, 1978). Empirical studies suggesting important criticisms of Piaget also include P. Bryant, *Perception and Understanding in Young Children*: *an Experimental Approach* (Methuen, 1974); I. J. Stone, H. T. Smith, and L. B. Murphy, eds., *The Competent Infant*: *Research and Commentary* (Basic Books, 1977); I. S. Siegel and C. J. Brainerd, eds., *Alternatives to Piaget*: *Critical Essays on the Theory* (Academic Press, 1978); C. J. Brainerd and many commentators, The Stage Question in Cognitive-Developmental Theory', in *The Behavioural and Brain Sciences*, 1 1978), pp. 173-214; and A. Burton and J. Radford, eds., *Thinking in Perspective*: *Critical Essays in the Study of Thought Processes* (Methuen, 1978).

The literature by and about Piaget is voluminous, and bibliographies appear as books in themselves. For example: *Catalogue des Archives Jean Piaget*, in French and English (University of Geneva, 1975); S. Modgil, ed., *Piagetian Research*: *A Handbook of Recent Studies* (NFER Publications, 1974); R. Droz and M. Rahmy, eds., *Understanding Piaget* (International Universities Press, 1972).

Chronology

1896	Born 9 August at Neuchâtel in Switzerland.
1907	First publication (about albino sparrow).
1915	Published religious prose-poem about war, *The Mission of the Idea*.
1918	Doctor of Natural Sciences, University of Neuchâtel (thesis on molluscs).
	Published semi-autobiographical novel, *Recherche*.
1919–20	Studied psychology and psychiatry, first at Zurich then Paris (with Binet).
1921	Director of Studies at Jean-Jacques Rousseau Institute in Geneva (education and child psychology).
1923	Marriage with Valentine Châtenay.
	Published first psychological book (LTC).
1925–9	Professor of Psychology, Sociology and Philosophy of the Sciences, University of Neuchâtel.
1925	Birth of daughter, Jacqueline.
1927	Birth of daughter, Lucienne.
1929–39	Associate Professor of History of Scientific Thought, University of Geneva.
1929–67	Director, International Bureau of Education.
1931	Birth of son, Laurent.
1933–71	Director, Institute for Educational Sciences, University of Geneva.
1936	Published first book on infant development (OIC).
1938–51	Professor of Psychology and Sociology, University of Lausanne.
1939–52	Professor of Sociology, University of Geneva.

1940–71   Professor of Experimental Psychology, University of Geneva.

1941   Published first book on concrete operations (CCN).

1947   Published first systematic statement of his psychology (PI).

1950   Published interdisciplinary work (IEG).

1952   Published autobiography (A).

1952–63   Professor of Developmental Psychology, Sorbonne.

1955   Published book on formal operations (GLT).

1955–   Director, International Centre for Genetic Epistemology, University of Geneva.

1971   Professor Emeritus, University of Geneva.